JIM PETERSEN

LIFESTYLE DISCIPLESHIP

The Challenge of Following Jesus in Today's World

NAVPRESS ◗
BRINGING TRUTH TO LIFE
NavPress Publishing Group
P.O. Box 35001, Colorado Springs, Colorado 80935

OUR GUARANTEE TO YOU

We believe so strongly in the message of our books that we are making this quality guarantee to you. If for any reason you are disappointed with the content of this book, return the title page to us with your name and address and we will refund to you the list price of the book. To help us serve you better, please briefly describe why you were disappointed. Mail your refund request to: NavPress, P.O. Box 35002, Colorado Springs, CO 80935.

The Navigators is an international Christian organization. Our mission is to reach, disciple, and equip people to know Christ and to make Him known through successive generations. We envision multitudes of diverse people in the United States and every other nation who have a passionate love for Christ, live a lifestyle of sharing Christ's love, and multiply spiritual laborers among those without Christ.

NavPress is the publishing ministry of The Navigators. NavPress publications help believers learn biblical truth and apply what they learn to their lives and ministries. Our mission is to stimulate spiritual formation among our readers.

© 1993 by Jim Petersen
Library of Congress Catalog Card Number: 93-39063
ISBN 08910-97759

Cover photo: © L. Prosor/SUPERSTOCK 1993

Some of the anecdotal illustrations in this book are true to life and are included with the permission of the persons involved. All other illustrations are composites of real situations, and any resemblance to people;e living or dead is coincidental.

Unless otherwise noted, Scripture quotations in this publication are taken from the *HOLY BIBLE: NEW INTERNATIONAL VERSION* (NIV). Copyright © 1973, 1978, 1984, International Bible Society. Used by permission of Zondervan Publishing House. All rights reserved. Other versions used include: the *New American Standard Bible (NASB)*, © The Lockman Foundation 1960, 1962, 1963, 1968, 1971, 1972, 1973, 1975, 1977; and the *King James Version (KJV)*.

Petersen, Jim.
    Lifestyle discipleship: the challenge of following Jesus in today's world/ Jim Petersen.
        p.   cm.
        Includes bibliographical references.
    ISBN 0-89109-775-9
    1. Spiritual formation. 2. Christian life—1960.
    I. Title.
    BV4501.2.P247   1993
    248.4—dc20   93-39063
                                                                      CIP

Printed in the United States of America
4 5 6 7 8 9 10 11 12 13/ 05 04 03 02 01 99

FOR A FREE CATALOG OF
NAVPRESS BOOKS & BIBLE STUDIES,
CALL 1-800-366-7788 (USA)
or 1-416-499-4615 (CANADA)

Contents

Overcoming Suffering and Adversity Through Faith
*Ministering When Others Experience Suffering
and Adversity*

This is for you, Dad.
Thanks for the godly heritage.

Preface

"For when David had served God's purpose
in his own generation, he fell asleep."[1]

The living room was full. Most of the people present had never
held a Bible in their hands until that moment. They had gathered at our home because they were parents—and their kids were
driving them crazy. The educated Brazilian is more Freudian than
anything else in his philosophy of child rearing. The prescription
is this: Don't repress your child's primitive instincts. Let him be
himself. If you restrict or discipline him, he will suffer for it the
rest of his life. Neurotics are adults with repressive childhoods.

Imagine never saying "no" to your three-year old! These people were frantic; a couple of the marriages were on the verge of
falling apart because they couldn't stand to live in the same house
with their own children. They were so desperate they were even
willing to resort to the Bible.

I passed the Bibles around the room. They were all alike so
that we could work by page numbers. I tried not to laugh. They
didn't quite know how to *hold* such an unusual book. They were
awkward with it—like it was something hot.

9

The first verse we looked at—the very first verse most had ever looked at in their lives—was Exodus 20:5—"For I, the LORD your God, am a jealous God, punishing the children for the sin of the fathers to the third and fourth generation of those who hate me." We read the verse and then I asked, "Do you think that's fair of God?" Several people in the room didn't believe God existed, but it didn't matter. Within five minutes of discussion, the entire group was united in their anger against this unfair God.

Then I asked them, "Do you want your children to grow up to be like you?" Again, they quickly reached a consensus. "No, life is pretty desperate for us—too much anxiety. We want better things for our children."

I then helped them see that Exodus 20:5 is a self-fulfilling prophecy. It's the way things work. Their kids will be exactly like them—unless they, as parents, do something to break the cycle.

Generations. Each one must harvest what their fathers planted, and each generation plants for their children. This particular harvest we are reaping probably wins the all-time record for difficulty. The social, economic, and philosophical revolutions of the past four centuries seem to have converged upon us at this point in history to give us a way of life that we're not so sure was made for human consumption.

But this is our generation, and as followers of Christ we are stewards of it. We can complain about the mess our ancestors left us, but that doesn't really do any good. Or we can revolt, just quit, refuse to have anything to do with it, and live our private little lives. But that would be irresponsible. There is another generation that is now in grade school, and they will keep coming until Christ returns. What are we to do?

Jesus' little story about the good seed among the weeds describes what I believe to be God's strategy for these times. He said, "The field is the world, and the good seed stands for the sons of the kingdom. The weeds are the sons of the evil one."[2] As sons and daughters of the Kingdom, our place for now is in the world, right there beside the sons of the evil one. We are there to germinate so that there will be a harvest, and seed for the next generation. It would be a calamity if we failed at this. There would be nothing left for our children but despair.

This book is about discipling—helping people know Christ and grow to be like Him within their present environments. Helping another person become like Christ breaks the cycle of hopeless living. It breaks it for that person and usually for his succeeding generations. The next verse in Exodus 20 continues, "but showing love to a thousand generations of those who love me and keep my commandments."[3]

Many outstanding books have been written on discipling, and I will be drawing from some of them as I go along. Almost nothing, however, has been written that addresses the subject within the context of our modern society. Change defines this society. Situations, lifestyles, beliefs, values, and even the way we think—all these exist in a state of change. The opportunities are unparalleled, but so are the complexities. Many Christians are confused and unsure of themselves. They don't understand the people they live and work with. The idea of sharing their faith seems so—*inappropriate*. Not knowing what else to do, they consign the entire responsibility for the spiritual needs of this generation to the church institutions. They pay the bills for the church programs and pray they will do the job.

This book is the third in a series on a single theme. The theme has to do with what we as God's people are to be and do if we are to fulfill God's purposes for us in our time and our culture—*in* the world.

The first book, *Living Proof*, deals with the matter of sharing our faith, especially with the people who are closest to us but often very far from Christ. It explains that evangelism is a process, and describes the mini-steps people usually must take in their move toward Christ. The book shows how we can assist people in this process.

Church Without Walls, the second book, explores the inevitable implications we will face as a church as we set out to reach unbelieving mainstream Americans. Since few of them will come to us, we must go to them. But at this point we run into a problem. Over the centuries we have become accustomed to having the traffic flow toward us. It has been pretty much a one-way street. come to and listen to. The state churches of the past established this mind-set, and we have never really broken the habit. *Church Without Walls* grapples with the matter of relearning how to get the traffic flowing in both directions once again.

This book, *Lifestyle Discipleship*, carries the subject further. What happens when we are successful in helping people of this generation come to Christ? As products of modernity, these people's lives have been built on lies rather than truth. Jesus, talking about Satan, said, "There is no truth in him. When he lies, he speaks his native language, for he is a liar and the father of lies."[4] To come to Christ is to step into the light of truth. To follow Him is to live the truth. That can be quite a stretch for many people, especially those who do not have the advantage of a Christian heritage. We must all begin our journey from wherever we happen to be when Christ calls us. This means we need to be able to serve people according to their ability, not according to our agenda. It also means we need to leave them in their context if they are to reach their peers. The purpose of this book is to equip people to serve others in this way.

NOTES
1. Acts 13:36.
2. Matthew 13:38.
3. Exodus 20:6.
4. John 8:44.

Acknowledgments

I knew this book was going to have to be written, but in my mind it was still a couple of years down the road. The response to the *Living Proof* video training series—produced by Christian Businessmen's Committee (CBMC), NavPress, and International Media Service—has accelerated the demand for this volume. The series was based on my book with the same title.

Living Proof addresses the subject of sharing our faith. This book deals with what happens after that. It addresses the questions people are asking about how to help the people coming to Christ grow to maturity. Since *Living Proof* is based on a set of assumptions that need to be carried on into the discipling process as well, there is an immediate need for this material.

I am indebted to my brothers at CBMC: Pat MacMillan, Joe Coggeshall, and Dave Stoddard. They convinced me that I needed to write this book now, and they also helped me greatly in putting it together. We had some wonderful brainstorming sessions together over it. Jake Barnett also gave me invaluable help by spending many hours working through the manuscript. Sue Gliebe has been another key person to this project. She drafted and redrafted the manuscript. I thank God for friends like these!

CHAPTER 1

Discipleship and Our Contemporary Culture

THIRTY YEARS OF DISCIPLESHIP PROGRAMS, AND WE ARE NOT DISCIPLED

If you have been around the Christian community at all, you know about discipleship. It is there on the right-hand side of the page of the church bulletin. The discipleship group meets on Tuesdays for breakfast at Underwood's Restaurant. In our bigger churches, we have pastors of discipleship. Our Christian bookstores always have a section reserved for discipleship materials. There you will find everything from a study booklet for new believers to complete courses in discipleship. Many of us have taken the course.

It was in the late 1950s that I first heard about discipleship. I was just getting started in my Christian life and was casting about trying to figure out how to make it work for me. Then I met some people who talked about Scripture memory, quiet times, and personal Bible study. One of them was Ed Reis. Their goals were to live as disciples of Jesus Christ and to multiply their numbers until they filled the world. It was heady stuff and I went after it.

I can't decide whether I was naive or arrogant in those days, but I was certainly mistaken. I believed the world would never be quite the same once this movement of discipleship had swept through it. Three decades have now passed. The gospel has done well in many parts of the world in these years. But in our Western society there has been a change in spiritual climate that is not at all what I had envisioned.

I didn't know it at the time—I wonder if anybody did—but a set of forces for change were already coming at us full speed. The storm had already begun to stir with the Economic Revolution of the Fifteenth Century. That was followed a couple of centuries later by the Industrial Revolution. Industry demanded urbanization, and our towns bulged into cities. Everyday life was changed forever for most Westerners. The Enlightenment, a simultaneous Philosophical Revolution, really added momentum to the storm. It elevated the scientific processes to the point that science had the last word on truth.

And so our beliefs and values had undergone a transformation. Succeeding revolutions in technology, communication, information and the *moving* of information, showered us with amenities our grandparents couldn't even dream of. Travel became easy, communication instant, and our homes became filled with gadgets too complicated for most of us to use. But the really big changes are to be found in our heads. It is impossible to experience this storm of modernization without being influenced in the way we think.

Modernization brought broad prosperity, relatively safe social systems, and a grand feeling of self-sufficiency. God became dispensable. People found that they could live very comfortably without Him, so that's what many of them did. As a nation, the USA cut itself loose from the moorings of the biblical religion that had been its foundation. Relativism, the notion that there are no absolutes, that there is no such thing as truth, became the prevailing belief. And since there was no truth, it really didn't matter what you believed as long as it helped you get through the day.

So all of us could believe whatever we want to—*but* whatever it is you believe in, be it God or the Great Pumpkin, keep it to yourself! Beliefs, we are told, should be kept private. And yet this privatization of our beliefs renders them quite useless. What good is a faith that you must leave at home? It won't help you or affect your behavior, nor will it do anyone else any good.

false assumption

it won't affect others in as powerful a way if it is privatized

This, in brief, is what the storm of modernization has done to our minds. The term for all of this is *modernity*. Modernity is a mind-set, a way of thinking. It is a way of thinking that eventually alienates. It cuts us adrift as a society, and on the individual level, life becomes an aimless wandering. What I am saying can be illustrated as follows.

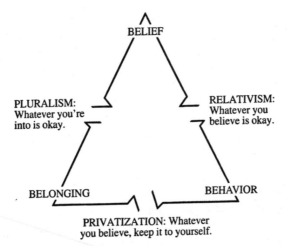

PRIVATIZATION: Whatever you believe, keep it to yourself.

Our beliefs become so tentative that they are not strong enough to bind us to others in community. We lose our capacity to belong. Because we don't belong, we have no accountability for our behavior. Our beliefs aren't strong enough to influence behavior either, so behavior goes out of control.

People who live this way get hurt.

TAKING STOCK OF OUR ASSUMPTIONS

There was a time when we thought we had discipleship figured out. But then this storm of change hit us, leaving us with a lot of unanswered questions. People have changed. Their beliefs have changed, their values have changed, and, most important of all, the manner in which they think has changed. These changes really constitute a general shift in the spiritual climate of the nation.

The first question we must ask is, Have our understanding and approaches to winning and discipling people accommodated these changes? How are we doing in our efforts among the people of modernity?

Many of our current practices for helping people follow Christ were formed in a context that is now vanishing from the scene. When the discipleship movement began several decades ago it was, by and large, an in-house affair. Most often it was one Christian helping another. Even most of the evangelism was done among people who had their roots in the church but had strayed. So everyone—the discipler, the disciple, and even the new Christian—shared a common heritage of beliefs and values. This natural affinity between all parties simplified everything.

My early experiences, which I briefly described at the beginning of this chapter, radically and permanently transformed my life. The individual, personal attention I received from Ed Reis over about a two-year period defined the rest of my life. Ed taught me how to pray and get answers, and how to study the Bible—how to read it, memorize it, and apply what I was learning to everyday life in practical terms. He taught me how to explain the gospel to people, and got me doing it. Most important, Ed gave me a vision for the potential of an individual who places himself or herself at God's disposal.

It didn't take long for me to recognize the value of people. I told my classmates about Christ and also began to help a few who were already Christians. I began to pass on to them the things I was learning. I was soon confronted with a problem of supply and demand. It seemed that all my Christian friends wanted to be "discipled." Others in my situation faced the same dilemma. There were many more people wanting attention than we could hope to help. The obvious solution was to become selective, to pick and choose. Of course we went for those who could make the greatest progress with the least effort on our part. We worked with the strong. The slogan was, "Move with the movers." Our rationale was, "We'll have more laborers more quickly this way." Our philosophy of discipleship was based on assumptions such as:

- Progress in discipleship is measured by a person's faithfulness in practicing certain disciplines *that we would prescribe.*
- People who falter or fail in these disciplines do so because they are halfhearted. They lack commitment. Or, they fail because they are pursuing other ungodly choices.
- People eliminate themselves from getting further attention by unfaithfulness of this sort. This frees us from further responsibility toward them.

his early assumptions

As I look at these assumptions now I feel embarrassed. They seemed good at the time, but they were only workable in an environment where everyone involved, from discipler to the new Christian, was really in the same context. We all understood the rules. Also, these things could only work where the supply and demand was in favor of the person doing the discipling.

I got an education a few years later when I found myself working as a missionary among Brazilian university students who didn't care about religion, much less discipleship! It took months and often years to lead one of those students into faith in Christ. After a yearlong struggle in endless hours of Bible study with an individual, I was not about to apply my "survival of the fittest" philosophy to that person. To the contrary! I was careful to adjust my expectations to reality. This meant I could encourage the person in whatever spiritual progress he was making. I realized that it had been easy for me to be tough on orphaned disciples, but with my own spiritual offspring I was far more gentle.

As things progressed over the succeeding years, I had to replace a number of other previously unquestioned assumptions about helping people grow in Christ. I watched the tide of supply and demand turn around, first in Europe and then in the US. The number of those hungry, highly motivated people who had been brought up in the church dwindled, in many places to a vanishing point. They were replaced by the people of modernity. Having given up on biblical religion and being quite convinced that there really was no such thing as truth, the idea of opening the Bible to look for truth made no sense to them at all. Christian campus organizations languished. Local churches began to feel the effects in more subtle ways. Attendance held fairly steady, but as people within the churches began to take on the mind-set of modernity, they suffered the consequences in their personal lives. Life began to fall apart for them, and many became emotionally disabled. Such people are not able to practice the disciplines we so often associate with discipleship. Even if they try, that usually isn't what they need.

Of course, there are multitudes of exceptions to this scenario. Thousands of Christians across the US continue to make following Christ the priority issue of their lives. They study and memorize the Scriptures, and seek to build their lives around them. But we would deceive ourselves if we took this fact as an indicator of what's happening in this country. The tide continues to move in the other direction as modernity claims the minds of more and more people inside and outside the church.

Before the enlightening experiences in Brazil, I had viewed discipleship as a system of information and disciplines that resulted in the mastering of a body of knowledge and a set of skills. So I organized a syllabus of information and how-tos, and busied myself with passing it on to the people I was helping. But something wasn't right. It finally dawned on me that I was forcing my agenda on everyone, and it didn't truly fit anyone. I needed to learn to begin at the other person's starting point. I describe this concept at length in *Living Proof* because this is one of the most basic principles for communicating the message of Christ to another person. The same rule extends into helping a person grow in Christ.

Indeed, the line between evangelizing a person and helping him follow Christ as a disciple is really unimportant. Too often we make too much of it. We say, "Now that you're a Christian . . ." and then we give him a shopping list of expectations. We would do far better, and the new believer would do far better, if we would simply continue doing the things that helped him find Christ in the first place: exploring the Scriptures together and talking about what they mean. The content will change, but the relationships and the environment should remain intact. The idea can be illustrated as follows:

OLD VIEW: Evangelism   Discipleship

NEW VIEW:
Discipleship
Evangelism

MINISTERING AMONG BROKEN PEOPLE

The church-oriented culture is aging and passing off the scene. It is being replaced by the people of modernity. Stability and security are not a part of their experience. They were raised in spiritual poverty and material affluence. More often than not they watched mom and dad split. They have been knocked around. Many live with profound fears and anxieties.

This description doesn't just apply to "those people who don't go to church." We who make up the church find ourselves swimming in this same soup along with the rest of society. Our TV sets are on, we read the magazines, take the same courses under the same professors, and work at the same jobs along with everyone else. We unwittingly take on the images our advertisers create for us. We pick up the mentality of our age, and soon it shows up in the way we think and act. Consequently, life has come apart for many of us within the church as well.

So those of us who aspire to help others know Christ and build their lives around Him and His truth need to reorient ourselves. The idea of sticking with the strong for the sake of efficiency has become something of a dead end. Such people are atypical. In their place we find the media-saturated relativist, who, more often than not, comes broken. The question we need to answer is, What does it take to see the broken made whole? That is one of the core questions we will be dealing with in this book.

JESUS AND BROKEN PEOPLE

Jesus described His work in terms of healing the broken. He came to give us the solution to the question we are asking. In Luke 4 we find Him returning to His hometown after being out and about in public ministry in the surrounding towns. The news of His extraordinary works had found their way back to Nazareth, so attendance was good at the synagogue that Sabbath morning.

At one point in the service, Jesus got up, took the scroll of Isaiah, and read out of it. It was a prophetic passage about the Messiah, whom every good Jew was expecting to appear. When He finished the reading, He said, "Today this scripture is fulfilled in your hearing."[1] He left no doubt. He was in essence saying, "I am the Messiah!"

That was a very interesting morning in the town of Nazareth, but of more interest to us here is the content of what He read. Let's look at the unabridged version out of Isaiah 61 from which Jesus read:

> The Spirit of the Sovereign LORD is on me,
>   because the LORD has anointed me
>   to preach good news to the poor.
> He has sent me to bind up the brokenhearted,
>   to proclaim freedom for the captives
>   and release from darkness for the prisoners,
> to proclaim the year of the LORD's favor
>   and the day of vengeance of our God,
> to comfort all who mourn,
>   and provide for those who grieve in Zion—
> to bestow on them a crown of beauty
>   instead of ashes,
> the oil of gladness
>   instead of mourning,
> and a garment of praise

instead of a spirit of despair.
They will be called oaks of righteousness,
  a planting of the LORD
  for the display of his splendor.
They will rebuild the ancient ruins
  and restore the places long devastated;
they will renew the ruined cities
  that have been devastated for generations.[2]

This is one of the most hope-inspiring passages in the entire Bible. We would do well to commit it to memory. Jesus is saying that the raw materials for His redemptive work are the poor, the heartbroken, and those who are enslaved. He will comfort such people and provide for them. He will exchange their sadness and despair for beauty and praise. He will not just heal them but transform them into "oaks of righteousness." Then they will be towers of strength and so He will put them to work rebuilding the ruins.

them —
or
us ?

Unbelievable!

Some people have claimed this passage as their proof text for giving priority to ministering to the materially poor and the politically oppressed. This diminishes the text and disproportionately elevates material injustices. Poverty comes in many forms. Who can say which kind hurts the most? God opposes oppression no matter what form it comes in, material or spiritual.

This American society of ours is certainly broken and in pain. We now know that modernity's promise, that progress is a road to paradise, is a lie. We were promised affluence and security but got fear and alienation instead.

Peggy Noonan, former speech writer for Ronald Reagan and George Bush, and former CBS news writer for Dan Rather, describes the angst we are talking about. She says, "Our ancestors believed in two worlds, and understood this to be the solitary, poor, nasty, brutish, and short one. We are the first generations of man that actually expected to find happiness here on earth, and our search for it has caused such—unhappiness. The reason: If you do not believe in another, higher world, if you believe only in the flat material world around you, if you believe this is your only chance at happiness—if that is what you believe, then you are not disappointed when the world does not give you a good measure of its riches; you are despairing."[3]

In our attempts to cope with this despair, we have created the therapist as our secular priest. His job is to help alleviate the pain. But he too tells us lies and will leave us broken still. His message is that it's all there inside yourself. He asserts that the individual must find and assert his or her true self because this self is the only source of genuine relationships with other people. One must know and accept one's self, he insists, in order to enter into valid relationships with others. One must become independent of others to come to where one doesn't need another's love to feel complete. People need self-validation, says the therapist. They need to be able to say, "I'm okay," independent of what others might think or say about them.

In contrast, Jesus calls our attention to the Cross, not to make us feel good about ourselves, but to make us realize that in spite of ourselves, all is forgiven. Rather than instructing us to shift the blame to our deprived childhood or abusive parents, He takes it all upon Himself, making it vanish forever. He holds us responsible for our own behavior because we are really the only ones who can do anything about it. He assures us that if we are willing, He will help us get started and also empower us to keep going.

Then He calls us into a set of interdependent relationships, with Himself and with our brothers and sisters. We are in these relationships, He says, not just for what we can get out of them, but also for what we can bring to them. Self-fulfillment is the wrong pursuit.

Healing, according to Jesus, is for those who are broken and admit it.

The incompatibility of these two messages—of the secular therapist and of Jesus—is almost total. Both cannot be true.

CONCLUSION

It is hard to imagine a greater challenge than the one I've just described. We now know the nature of the storm and what it has deposited on our doorstep. Modernization supplies us with unprecedented resources and opportunities. We can connect with people and communicate in ways we never dreamed possible. Modernity, on the other hand, is leaving us with a world of damaged people who have lost their notion of truth, and with it their sense of transcendence.

How are we going to respond to this hour? Will it be business as usual, or will we get ourselves ready to seize the opportunity? We need to reexamine our basic assumptions about discipleship against the Scriptures, in light of our contemporary situation.

QUESTIONS FOR THOUGHT

1. Can you see where modernity has influenced the way you live and think?

2. What influences has modernity had on your Christian life?

3. Do you hold assumptions about relating to other people in the area of your faith that may need to change in light of this chapter? What are some of them?

NOTES
1. Luke 4:21.
2. Isaiah 61:1-4.
3. Peggy Noonan, "You'd Cry Too If It Happened to You," *Forbes* (September 14, 1992), vol. 150, number 6, page 65.

CHAPTER 2

Insiders

A s our society abandons its foundations of biblical religion and gropes its way toward neo-paganism, certain things become obvious. For one, the distance between biblical truth and modernity's mind-set is widening. Truth of any kind, even the kind that science can offer, is being rejected. Gross contradictions are in. People are creating their own designer religions, and if we happen to object on the basis of reason, it is *we* who are the bigots. America is as religious as ever, but we are changing gods.

What this means in practical terms is that our basic strategy for connecting with the unbelieving world is going to have to change. Until now, our assumption has been that somehow, sooner or later, we can manage to get them to come to us. That assumption is becoming increasingly unrealistic. A certain percentage will come, perhaps enough to keep us distracted and even feeling successful, but the vast majority will not. For them, what we do in church is irrelevant.

When we find ourselves confronted by a critical issue such as this one, we need to return to Scripture to search for the answers. Our first step in this search is to decide exactly what we're looking for. We need to formulate our question. In this case, our question should be, How are God's people supposed to relate to the unbelieving world around them?

We begin our study in the Old Testament. We ask, How did Israel relate to the unbelieving world? We soon discover that Israel *was* God's message, His vehicle of communication to the rest of the nations. Their message was in their uniqueness, as they lived by the civil, ceremonial, and moral laws God had given them through Moses.[1] They were not to mix with their neighbors in marriage, or take on their customs, because such a mixture would blur God's image.[2]

The plan was not to send Israel into the world to reach the nations. Rather, He planted her in the world to attract the nations. That plan worked as long as Israel was faithful.[3]

The New Testament opens on a very different note. Israel had fallen into dishonor in the eyes of the nations. Yet Jesus came as a member of this discredited people. He offered Himself to them, but they rejected Him. What we often fail to understand was that He came to the Jews, confined His ministry to them for the sake of the nations of the world.[4]

God's purpose for His people was not to restore their national splendor so that the world would again be attracted to them. Rather, He focused on the few, capitalized on their heritage, revealed to them who He was, and scattered them into the world.[5] The fruit of this scattering was a new people: the church.

There is a basic difference in strategy for God's people of the Old Testament and His people of the New. Rather than the *come and see* of the Old, it is now, *go to and live among*. It is as critical now as it was in Old Testament times that we live holy lives. Ungodly living will destroy us and our credibility just as surely now as it did then. But we are to live our lives *among* the lost rather than separated from them. God's people today are a people sent; we are to *go to and live among*. So, a basic difference between the calling of God's people in the Old and New Testaments is that the arrows have been turned around. Where it was once *come* _and see_, it is now "go to and proclaim."[6] It seems we are having difficulty getting out of the Old Testament and into the New in understanding what we're to be about.

[handwritten margin note: none of us has lived OT]

One of the key players in this New Testament strategy is the "insider." An interesting description of this person is found in 1 Corinthians 7.

The first-century Christians of Corinth had been converted out of paganism. But as they struggled their way out of their grave clothes, Paul had to help them get untangled. They constantly fought losing battles with worldliness, giving in to jealousy and quarrels among themselves. They bickered over which of their leaders was the greatest: Paul, Apollos, or Peter.

The Corinthian believers tolerated an incestuous relationship in their midst, while others among them questioned whether even married believers should have sexual relations. They had a hard time getting away from idolatrous practices and temptations to sexual immorality. They took each other to court. And in spite of all of their weaknesses, Paul had to warn them repeatedly against their arrogance and boasting. Incredibly, some even doubted Paul's motives in going to them, wondering if he wasn't in it for the money!

Their problems are our problems today, so it is not a very long stretch to go from his instructions to a contemporary application. They, like us, were a minority in a pagan society. But the strategy that Paul prescribes is strikingly different from ours. In fact, what he advocates invades the comfort zone of many of us.

CALLED TO SERVE AS INSIDERS

When people first come to Christ, they are often encouraged to make immediate radical changes in their life situations in order to do God's will. There is a pervasive attitude among us that makes it the norm for new believers to deliberately withdraw from their old friends, their families, and all their old associations until eventually they are living in virtual isolation from everything but their new Christian community.

Paul addresses a similar problem in chapter 7 of 1 Corinthians. Apparently the Christians, because of the pressures on their faith, were making unwise decisions in major areas of life. Some found themselves married to unbelieving spouses and were contemplating divorce. Others were wondering about changing their religious-cultural identities and were thinking they should get circumcised. Some felt trapped in their jobs as slaves and had anxieties over how to serve both God and an earthly master at the same time.

Paul's instructions on these matters are surprising. On the matter of unequal marriage he says: "Each one should retain the place in life that the Lord *assigned to him* and *to which God has called him.*"[7] On the question of religious-cultural identity he makes an almost identical statement: "Each one should *remain* in the situation which he was in *when God called him.*"[8] On the bad job he said the same: "Each man, as responsible to God, should *remain* in the situation God *called* him to."[9]

These repetitive statements make it clear that when people come to Christ, as a rule *they are already positioned to serve God.* They have already found their place. They just need to recognize that.

We live in a highly mobile society where job changes and relocations are the norm. Paul is not suggesting that it is wrong to move, change jobs, or in some cases to alter our marital status. He encourages the slave to take his freedom if he can get it. There are good reasons for changing jobs or getting married. However, finding a "real ministry" is not one of them. God does sometimes call people to leave the job and sell the house to go do a specific task, but that is the exception rather than the rule.

Where to serve is among the first issues in our call to discipleship. We are to serve Christ as insiders in an unbelieving world. Many of us have withdrawn from our old associations to where we have all but lost our insidership. In a sense we have abandoned a post that was uniquely ours, that cannot be filled by another in exactly the same way. So a part of discipleship is learning how to fulfill Christ's purposes for us in our everyday situation.

THE MAIN CHARACTER

The insider is the main character in this book. He was one of the keys to God's purposes in the first century and is every bit as important to His purposes in this generation. Ironically, though the insider is a main character, he has been seriously neglected. We hardly ever talk about him. Maybe that's because we don't even think about him or we don't know what to say. Our experiences as insiders have been meager, and often disappointing. So perhaps we are just ignoring the subject.

This book was written to encourage you to be an insider, to bear fruit in those circles that are uniquely yours, and also to help equip you to empower others as insiders.

CALLED TO DO WHAT?

The natural question at this point is to ask, If we are called as insiders to our present situation, what is it we are supposed to do? A familiar church catechism says our job here on earth is to glorify God. There are many passages throughout Scripture that support that statement. Isaiah writes:

"Bring my sons from afar
    and my daughters from the ends of the earth—
everyone who is called by my name,
    whom I created for my glory,
    whom I formed and made."[10]

I struggled for years to grasp the meaning of that statement and its practical implications. If we trace Jesus' use of the word *glorify* through the Gospel of John, it becomes apparent that glorifying God means revealing something about Him so that people can see Him more clearly. Jesus told His Father, "I have brought you glory on earth by completing the work you gave me to do. . . . I have revealed you to those whom you gave me."[11] In the same way, God intends that through us, nonChristians will see Him and believe. He intends that those who do believe will be inspired to know Him better as they see His person reflected in us.

So we are called to reveal God to believers and unbelievers alike in the context of our families, friendships, and jobs. This is precisely what Jesus was getting at when He said, "You are the salt of the earth . . . you are the light of the world. A city on a hill cannot be hidden. Neither do people light a lamp and put it under a bowl. Instead they put it on a stand. . . . Let your light shine before men, that they may see your good deeds and praise your father in heaven."[12]

WHAT ABOUT OUR CALL TO SEPARATION FROM THE WORLD?

Not much is being taught about this matter of our being insiders. More often the instructions run in the opposite direction. We are more likely to hear that the world is a dangerous place and we need to keep our distance. There is truth to that! Further on, in Paul's same letter to the Corinthians, he penned the words, "Do not be misled: 'Bad company corrupts good character.' "[13] So we must ask, What do we have here—contradictory counsel? In the first case Paul instructs his fellow believers to remain in their present situation, and later he tells them to stay away from bad company. What do we do if our present situation is filled with bad company?

Obviously, there are situations that are so bad that the first thing a new believer must do is get out. I have a friend who was in the Mafia when he came to Christ. For him the question was not whether or not he should get out, but how to get out and stay alive. My dad is studying the Bible with a drug dealer. That man will soon need to look for a new livelihood. But these are the exceptions.

The confusion is in our understanding of what constitutes keeping one's distance. We often interpret it to mean we are to have nothing to do with the people who live ungodly lives. A distinction needs to be made here. We are instructed to "have nothing to do with the fruitless deeds of darkness."[14] The distinction is between the unbelieving *person* and his *deeds*. We are ınstructed to love the unbeliever. We are told to be wise in our relationships with unbelievers so that we can make the most of every opportunity.[15]

Keeping ourselves pure is not really a matter of our physical proximity to evil. It is a matter of our minds being conformed to God and His Word. Jesus prayed to His Father concerning His disciples, "My prayer is not that you take them out of the world but that you protect them from the evil one. . . . Sanctify them by the truth; your word is truth. As you have sent me into the world, I have sent them into the world. For them I sanctify myself, that they too may be truly sanctified."[16]

Jesus was the original insider. He came and lived among us. Sinners gathered around Him. His purpose for His disciples was that they too should serve as insiders. He sent them into the world in the same way that His Father sent Him. So it is with us as well. We need to live as insiders in the same manner that Jesus did.

NOBODY DOES IT ALONE

This image of the insider we have just described could be misleading if we do not put it into a broader biblical perspective. We are a society of individualists and we like it that way. The pages of our history books present a parade of people who with their own two hands fought wars, forged governments, built industries, and made fortunes. It's "the American way." Frank Sinatra was only half joking when he introduced his autobiographical song, "I Did It My Way," as our national anthem.

We carry this pride in individual achievement over into our response to God's calling as well. When we hear the familiar command, "Go make disciples," a Lone Ranger image comes up on our screen: riding out to evangelize and disciple, and then coming back in with another notch on his gun. If that is the picture you are operating on, I assure you, you will try and most of you will fail, and then you will very possibly spend the rest of your life doing little or nothing among unbelieving people.

I have a friend who loves God and aches to bear fruit among the many people he knows. He is a true insider. He is also a very busy man. The last time I saw him he told me he had managed to put a Bible study together for some of his friends. They were meeting *once a month* and it was killing him.

I tried to help him think through some people he could team up with who could supplement what he was doing with their energy and gifts. He wouldn't hear of it. That was his deal and those were his friends and he was going to do this thing by himself.

The truth that every believer is interdependent with his or her brothers and sisters is at the core of the very definition of God's people. Each of us has been given the Holy Spirit, who in turn has given us spiritual gifts. We're supposed to use those gifts to serve one another. The major passages in the New Testament on the church underscore this truth.[17]

In 1 Corinthians 12 Paul uses the analogy of the human body to make the point. The body is a unit, he says, made up of many parts. The foot cannot say, "Because I am not a hand, I do not belong to the body." Nor should the ear say, "Because I am not an eye, I do not belong to the body. . . . God has arranged the parts in the body, each one of them, just as he wanted them to be."[18] Can you imagine a big ear out there attempting to act like a whole body!

It should come as a great relief to discover we aren't supposed to try to go it alone, that God has designed us in such a way that we must depend on one another.

In my work situation I am one of a team of four. The workload is heavy because we're overseeing a global society that involves about ninety countries. Each of the four of us is very different from the others, and that's what makes us effective. When something comes to us, we decide which of us should do it based on who is good at that sort of thing. So we work together out of our strengths and cover for one another's weaknesses. This allows us to accomplish a lot of work, and have fun doing it.

In my activities as an insider the same principle applies. To begin with, my wife and I do everything together, again according to our strengths. We have several sets of relationships in which people are in various stages of knowing Christ and growing in Him. Some are neighbors, others revolve around our children and their friends, and so on.

With everything else that is going on in our lives, I wouldn't have time to be involved in even one of these situations if I had it in my mind that it was all up to me. Since every effort is understood to be a team effort, I am free to do what I can and count on the others to do the rest.

IMPERFECT PEOPLE HELPING IMPERFECT PEOPLE

We are called to be insiders in whatever station of life we find ourselves, but we cannot discharge this calling all by ourselves. We need to be teamed with brothers and sisters who can compensate for what we lack. This truth gets us past a major obstacle on this road we're on: our personal limitations.

Too many Christians of our generation are basically sitting out the game in the bleachers. Some will help with the in-house chores around the church, but when the action moves toward the unbeliever, they slip back into the stands. Paul describes Epaphroditus as his brother, fellow worker and fellow soldier.[19] We have many brothers and sisters, and a few fellow workers. But fellow soldiers are very scarce indeed! Why is this the case?

Many of us feel so inadequate and unprepared that we simply consider ourselves to be unqualified. We say, "I have nothing to offer. My own life is in disarray. My marriage is in trouble. I'm worried about my kids. Financially we're barely making ends meet. I've got to retrain to hold my job. I'm fighting a losing battle against calories. My relationship with Christ isn't exactly transforming my own life. What do I have that anyone else would even want? Besides, I'm so busy I can't even think about taking on more."

It is true that many Christians live lives that seem to be unmarked by Christ's presence. It is possible to belong to Christ but remain a spiritual infant. Paul asked the Corinthians, "Are you not worldly? Are you not acting like mere men?"[20] Mere men! This seems to imply that a mature believer is something more than a mere mortal.

But it is also true that many Christians who consider themselves unfit and feel they have nothing to offer have, in fact, great potential for ministering to others. True, they are still in the thick of it with their personal battles. They can't refer to their struggles in the past tense because they lost a round just yesterday. "How can I," they ask, "help others in areas where I am still fighting losing battles?"

There is a big difference between these people and the others we described. The chronic infant has made peace with the enemy, while this second group is seeking to come to grips with their problems and to be delivered from them. They are looking to the Spirit of God for help, and trying to live by biblical truth. They pray their way through their struggles. They don't have many answers to their prayers to show others, and there aren't many final victories to talk about. But the significant thing about these people is that they are battling. They are fighting the very same battles their "mere men" brothers and sisters have written off as unwinnable. More significant, they are fighting against the same issues that are victimizing their unbelieving family and friends. People can identify with them.

Most all of us, Christian or not, must cope with broken relationships that marked us in childhood, job insecurity, children who are being enticed into destructive behavior, and days that have only twenty-four hours.

We do live in a stressful, chaotic world. The only people who seem to deny it are the Christians who still insist that "every day with Jesus is sweeter than the day before." I know I have had some very bad days in the forty years I have been following Him. So has every other Christian I know. It's just hard for us to come clean and admit it. We're afraid that if we tell it like it is, we'll ruin our testimony. What we fail to understand is that our refusal to bring to light what we really are, to be honest about our sins, fears, and struggles, leaves us with no testimony at all.

I have a Christian friend who fought a losing battle with several personal habits and unholy values for years. Finally he decided to get serious about dealing with them. Part of his solution was to become transparent according to James 5:16—"Confess your sins to each other and pray for each other so that you may be healed." Neither he nor anyone else anticipated the response. People seek him out day and night. He is one of the most fruitful people I know.

Why do broken people seek him out, and why is he so successful at helping them get to know God? First of all, people with problems know he understands. They know that at the very least they'll get a compassionate ear, not a condescending pat on the head from someone whose life appears to have been sanitized. But second, they also know he's making progress, even though it's slow, in overcoming his problems. He has hope, and he's getting somewhere. Hope is a rare commodity in our world, and if you have it, people want to know where you got it. People want to know what you're doing right, or where you're getting help.

When strugglers call him, my friend lets them know he's a fellow struggler. He listens, cares, and doesn't fill them with advice. Instead, he just tells them what he's doing and what he knows so far about what God is doing with him. They draw their own conclusions. He'll stay up late to just talk, pray, or study the Bible with someone if that will help. But he refuses to become anyone's guru. Believers and unbelievers alike go to him. Some know the Bible far better than he does, but he has something they do not: the freedom that comes from honesty.

CONCLUSIONS

We are called by God to serve Him as insiders to our normal life situations. We fulfill that calling as we glorify Him. We glorify Him as we reflect the character of Christ among believers and unbelievers alike.

We are not of the world, but our designated position is in the world. Our safety from evil is not a matter of withdrawing, but of sanctifying our minds through Christ and His Word.

If we are to move beyond just being present as insiders to the place where we become involved in people's lives to help them become followers of Christ, we're going to need help. We will need to team up with others who can fill in the gaps for us.

Modernity has compounded the complexity of our task as

insiders. Our world is chaotic. We live with pressures and insecurities of all sorts. Most of us struggle with financial worries. We are nervous about job security. Family relationships are often strained to the breaking point. We wonder if we haven't already alienated our kids. We've joined the "crime watch" and wonder if we shouldn't go out and buy a gun. Then we watch the news and wonder if there's a single spot in the world that's not falling apart.

Our time-saving inventions have not saved us any time at all. They have just increased the velocity of life. Gone are the days when you could drop a letter in the mail with the knowledge that it would be at least five days before a reply would come and you'd have to think about that matter again. The fax machine and its cousins make it all happen right now. So time has become our most precious commodity. We have no margin, no extra space, in our lives.

What we have been saying can be illustrated as follows:

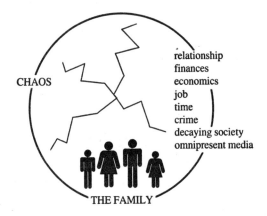

We all, Christian and nonChristian alike, live in the same environment. It is to this common world that we who believe are called to serve as insiders. This constitutes both a problem and an opportunity. It is a problem to the extent that living itself can consume us. Our hands can be more than full just coping with our own private chaos. But this same chaos becomes an opportunity as we learn to survive. By learning to apply biblical wisdom and to rely on spiritual resources, we can live balanced, meaningful lives in the midst of it all. When this happens, the gospel starts to look increasingly attractive to those who are watching.

Finally, when we think about discipling people in such a context, we must recognize the need to deal with their contemporary life issues in biblical, practical ways. We cannot pretend these issues do not exist. We would simply add another burden to already overburdened people if we chose an agenda unrelated to their needs. The degree to which we are able to apply God's truth to today's issues will determine what kind of deliverance the people we reach out to will experience.

QUESTIONS FOR THOUGHT

1. Describe situations in your life where you are or can become an insider.

2. What opportunities do they offer to minister to people?

3. What kind of help could you use in your efforts to be fruitful as an insider? Who could provide it?

4. Can you identify with the author's observations about chaos? Why?

5. Can you imagine making the chaos work in favor of God's purposes?

NOTES
1. Deuteronomy 4:5-9.
2. Exodus 18:3-5.
3. 1 Kings 10:24.
4. See Romans 15:8-12.
5. See John 17.
6. 1 Peter 2:9-12.
7. 1 Corinthians 7:17.
8. 1 Corinthians 7:20.
9. 1 Corinthians 7:24.
10. Isaiah 43:6-7.

11. John 17:4,6
12. Matthew 5:13-16.
13. 1 Corinthians 15:33.
14. Ephesians 5:11.
15. Colossians 4:5.
16. John 17:15-19.
17. See 1 Corinthians 12; Romans 12:4; Ephesians 4:7-16; 1 Peter 4:10.
18. 1 Corinthians 12:14-18.
19. Philippians 2:25.
20. 1 Corinthians 3:3.

CHAPTER 3

Things that Are Timeless:
The Goals of Spiritual Growth

Modernity is a way of thinking that cuts people adrift from truth, from community, and from a sense of personal responsibility for their behavior. Modernity fragments. It only breaks up society and leaves the individual broken as well. Those of us who are serious about being fruitful in helping people know Christ and grow into His likeness will have to deal with this fragmentation.

As the people of modernity move further and further away from biblical truth, the possibility of their coming to us grows increasingly remote. God intends that the insider be a key player in His purposes in the world, and at this juncture the insider is truly indispensable.

Insiders are the men or women who, in the normal course of life, establish sets of relationships that are uniquely theirs. Every person is an insider, and for the great majority of us, that should be the main arena of our service. The sad reality is that few of us manage to make much of the opportunities that are there for us as insiders.

We have not made the equipping of insiders a matter of priority. We have relied instead on calling people to "come join us," making this our basic strategy for reaching the unbeliever.

Another problem comes out of our individualism. We think we can do it alone out there, but we can't. Every insider needs others to help fill the gaps in the areas of time, experience, and gifting. He or she needs to be part of a team, and needs coaching—lots of coaching, by people who have already played the game. The primary purpose of this book is to encourage Christians to become or remain insiders and to help equip them to be fruitful in their place of service.

Therefore, let's turn our attention to the question of goals as we seek to help people know Christ. Exactly what do we want to accomplish?

The fascinating thing about the subject of this chapter is that it is timeless, virtually unaffected by the winds of change we've been talking about thus far. This chapter would be suitable for any generation of the past two thousand years. Societies change, people change, but God's purposes remain unwavering through it all. We do not change the truths of the gospel to fit the hearer, or the society. To do that would be to distort the gospel, and a distorted gospel is really no gospel at all.[1]

What needs changing is the manner in which we serve people with the good news. If we impose personal or cultural conditions on the gospel, people will often simply go the other way. If we use language that is difficult to understand, or speak of things irrelevant to what life is all about for people, they will not listen. However, before we can begin to adjust to meet the needs of people, we need to be very clear on two things:

- Our role in the lives of the people we help.
- Our primary goals as we help them know and follow Christ.

OUR ROLE: A "PARENTAL" RESPONSIBILITY

By far the most common metaphor used in the New Testament to describe the basic relationship involved in bringing people to maturity in Christ is that of parent and child. Almost all the writers of the Epistles describe their work in these terms.

Paul writes, "My dear children, for whom I am again in the pains of childbirth until Christ is formed in you."[2] To the believers in Thessalonica he writes, "But we were gentle among you, like a mother caring for her little children . . . for you know that we dealt with each of you as a father deals with his own children, encouraging, comforting and urging you to live lives worthy of God."[3] The Apostle Peter wrote, "Like newborn babies, crave pure spiritual milk, so that by it you may grow up in your salvation, now that you have tasted that the Lord is good."[4] The Apostle John repeatedly addressed those he wrote to as "dear children,"[5] and the writer of Hebrews talks about spiritual infancy and the importance of moving on to adulthood.[6]

What Does It Mean?

Metaphors can be misleading. It is very easy to carry them out beyond their intended meaning to reach our own independent conclusions. Then we risk stepping beyond truth. So we must ask, What is the obvious meaning of this metaphor? To me it describes the attitude a person should have toward the people he or she is helping walk with Christ.

Watch a new mother with a new baby. Words like "attentive" and "giving" come to mind. The mother's personal needs and desires come second. A mother is alert to her children's needs, giving each one appropriate, individualized attention. It is an attitude that results in a strong, positive relationship.

Our tendency is to create programs for discipleship and offer them to people as a substitute for parental care. We put people through a prescribed curriculum and expect that to take care of their needs. It doesn't work. It doesn't work because their primary need at this stage is not for information. Caring relationships are far more important to the early stages.

New Christians need a meaningful relationship with spiritual parents. It's a primary spiritual need, along with their need for Scripture. If study guides are used, they need to be carefully chosen. They must guide people into Scripture, and the content of those study guides must truly correspond with needs. If we fail to connect in these matters of relationships and appropriate content, the new Christian will often just stall out in his or her growth. They might do the studies and show up with all the right answers but still flunk the test in true spiritual growth.

What It Doesn't Mean

I have seen people extend this idea of spiritual parenthood to the point where one person virtually takes over the life of another. This kind of control becomes bizarre and creates dependency rather than producing adulthood. Paul said, "Not that we lord it over your faith, but we work with you for your joy, because it is by faith you stand firm."[7] We commit people to weakness when we assume excessive responsibility in their lives. They must learn to stand firm by their faith, not by ours.

OUR PRIMARY GOALS
IN HELPING PEOPLE FOLLOW CHRIST

The parent-child relationship forms the basic context for spiritual growth. Now the question is, Where are we headed with this relationship? What are we trying to accomplish?

Laying the Foundation

The Apostle Paul uses another metaphor to respond to this question. He believed his job was to lay foundations. He would arrive in a city, bring some people into faith in Christ, help them get sufficiently established so they could stand on their own, and then he would move on. He would leave it for others, primarily people from within that fledgling nucleus, to complete the superstructure and do the finishing work. He said, "I laid a foundation as an expert builder, and someone else is building on it. But each one should be careful how he builds. For no one can lay any foundation other than the one already laid, which is Jesus Christ."[8]

The way he phrased that doesn't leave much room for debate. No relativity in that statement! Either you have Christ for your foundation, or you have nothing at all! Why is that?

When we stop and think about the great truths that comprise the gospel we must quickly acknowledge that they are of such magnitude that they do indeed leave no space for anything else. If the gospel is true, then all other ideas must take their places around it. Any single facet of the gospel is, in itself, overwhelming. And when taken together, if we really believe all these facets to be true, they can have only one effect: They will turn our lives around. They will become our magnetic pole, our True North.

Consider! God, the Creator of the universe, entered time and space as a man—as one of our own species. He lived among us, and we could watch Him, listen to Him, and test Him with questions.

This God-man, Jesus of Nazareth, traveled through His life with a single purpose. This purpose was declared up front, at one of His first public appearances. He was identified as the "Lamb of God who takes away the sin of the world."[9] Every single person among those He came to was familar with the idea of a lamb being used for sacrifice. This man was God's sacrifice. He was there to be killed. It was either Him or us that would have to die, and God, out of incomprehensible love, made the choice we would never ever have made if it were us doing the choosing.

Consider the Resurrection: Early one morning on an otherwise ordinary day, this man got up off the stone His body had been laid out on three days earlier. And He walked out of there. If that happened, if it really happened, our perspective on our very existence must reflect that event. We will live with a sense of transcendence that will alter *everything*.

A handful of men stood gaping as the man they had followed for several years started rising up into the sky and disappeared ("the ascension"). Where did Christ go and where is He now? What is He doing? Well, right now He's in many places. He is in you—if you are His. And He is also in "the inner sanctuary, behind the curtain."[10] That means Christ is, right now, at work guaranteeing our position: reserving a place for us, and making sure we will not be carried off in the meantime.[11]

There are other great truths that we should mention here, but these four are at the core of what we believe. Christ is the central figure in all of them. Indeed, the entire Bible is so intensely Christ-centered that to remove Him from its text would leave us with nothing. He is the foundation. He is also the superstructure that goes on the foundation. We are to be "rooted and built up in him."[12]

Raising the Superstructure

In 1 Corinthians 13:13 Paul says that the effects of this message can be summarized in three words: faith, hope, and love. As we trace these three words through the Epistles, it becomes apparent that the writers assessed their ministries and the progress of their spiritual offspring with the question: How are they doing in the areas of faith, hope, and love? If these three virtues were evident, they were satisfied and the letter would go on to encourage them to continue to grow in the direction they were already headed. If they were getting off track or if something was missing in these areas, the letter would deal with the particular problem.

Years ago I heard Dr. Gene Getz illustrate this out of 2 Thessalonians. In chapter 1, verse 3, Paul commends the believers as he does in all of his letters. Usually he commends them for their faith, hope, and love. But here he says, "Your faith is growing more and more, and the love every one of you has for each other is increasing." That was it. He didn't mention hope. That was because some people had been tampering with their hope. The purpose of the letter was to help them get their hope back in place. So chapter 2 starts out, "Concerning the coming of our Lord Jesus Christ and our being gathered to him . . . don't become easily unsettled or alarmed by some prophecy . . . saying the day of the Lord has already come." Then he proceeds to set the record straight in order to restore their hope.[13]

Why this focusing on these three virtues—faith, hope, and love? What about the rest? Why not make it obedience, purity, and endurance? There are two reasons. First, faith, hope, and love are proof that the great truths about Christ have really taken hold in a person's life. And second, where there is faith, hope, and love you will soon have all the rest as well.

Faith, Hope, and Love—and the Gospel

Faith has its origins in Christ. The writer of the letter to the Hebrews exhorts us to "fix our eyes on Jesus, the author and perfecter of our faith."[14] We have staked our destinies on the idea that Jesus of Nazareth was in fact God, and that His death and resurrection resolves the problem of our alienation from God.

Our *hope* is in Christ's resurrection and ascension. Peter writes, "In his great mercy he has given us new birth into a living hope through the resurrection of Jesus Christ from the dead."[15] And in Hebrews we read, "We have this hope as an anchor for the soul, firm and secure. It enters the inner sanctuary . . . where Jesus, who went before us, has entered on our behalf."[16]

Love: Where does love originate? The Apostle John writes, "This is how we know what love is: Jesus Christ laid down his life for us."[17]

So faith, hope, and love are the outworking of Christ's incarnation, death, burial, resurrection, and ascension. The sprouting of these three virtues in the lives of new believers are the first signs of true spiritual life. When they are in full bloom, all of the other virtues will also be in evidence as well.

Faith, Hope, and Love: The Origins of All the Rest

The Apostle Paul begins his letter to the Christians in Thessalonica with the words, "We always thank God for all of you. . . . We continually remember before our God and father your *work* produced by faith, your *labor* prompted by love, and your *endurance* inspired by hope in our Lord Jesus Christ."[18] There is a cause and effect relationship between faith, hope, and love and every other virtue.[19]

Faith produces good works. It also produces perseverance,[20] courage, sacrificial concern for others,[21] and freedom.[22] It defeats Satan [23] and prompts us to worship.[24] The list could go on.

Hope not only motivates us to endure; it keeps us pure[25] and makes us bold with God.[26] It stabilizes us,[27] brings joy,[28] gives us a transcendental perspective,[29] and keeps us strong while in the midst of trials.[30] Again, there is more we could add.

Some of the fruits of love are: forgiveness,[31] obedience,[32] service to others,[33] unity and harmony,[34] patience, kindness, and humility.[35]

There is a lot more, but you get the picture. If there is faith, hope, and love, everything else will eventually be there too. And the presence of these three virtues evidences the fact that we have truly grasped the gospel and that it has taken root in us. What we have been saying can be illustrated as follows:

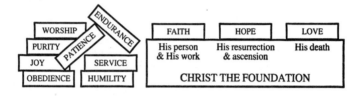

SUMMARY

We pursue our goal of helping people follow Christ by bringing them into an understanding of the great truths concerning Christ and His work, and how those truths are to be worked out in the way they live their lives. The promise of the gospel is that it will produce in us every conceivable virtue. Faith, hope, and love are the fountainheads of these virtues. The objective is to help people live by this gospel in every circumstance of life.

Connecting the Gospel to the Issues of Life

The truths we have just examined are more than adequate for dealing with whatever problems or dilemmas we might find ourselves in. But it is so easy to be wayward, to stray from the simplicity of God's truth and wander into another "truth" of our own making. Paul worried out loud to his offspring in Corinth over this. "I am afraid, lest as the serpent deceived Eve by his craftiness, your minds should be led astray from the simplicity and purity of *devotion* to Christ."[36]

What Paul feared for the Christians in Corinth has come upon us today. Somewhere along the line, these truths have gotten uncoupled from life. The cause and effect is often gone. The truths are there—in our heads—but they no longer transform us. We vow our allegiance to the God who lived among us, died in our place, and assumed authority over every conceivable power. Yet when it comes to dealing with the affairs of everyday life or resolving our problems, we proceed as if He had not come at all. We fail to make the connection between Christ's work and our needs. Truth has lost its effect on practice. This, I believe, is the great tragedy that has impoverished so many of us who bear Christ's name today.

When it comes to the practical outworking of an issue, we repeatedly resort to other voices, whether it is in our understanding and exercising of leadership, the manner in which we deal with the social issues of our day, or our notions of progress and success—to name a few.

David Powlison has written a very thought-provoking chapter for the book *Power Religion* that illustrates my point. It is titled "Integration or Inundation." He deals with the popularization of psychology within evangelicalism.

Powlison maintains that historically evangelical churches and theologians have failed to grapple with the problems in living that are inevitable to human experience. We have either ignored the real needs of everyday life, or we have oversimplified their solution with pietisms such as "Let go and let God," or "Die to self."[37]

Modern psychology has come in to fill the vacuum created by this lapse. Powlison says, "In this past quarter century we have witnessed the creation of a 'Christian mental health establishment' under the banner statement, 'the integration of psychology and Christianity.'"[38] One evidence of this is to be found on the shelves of Christian bookstores that overflow with popular self-help books. "This mass movement," he charges, "is not a theoretical attempt to integrate psychology and Christianity. It is an overt psychologization of the faith and life of professedly Christian people."[39]

What we have lost in this transfer of confidence to the psychologist is our belief that the gospel does address the deepest needs of the human experience. It shows we have forgotten what we have in the gospel. One unattended task that awaits us is to go into the Scriptures with our list of twenty-first-century problems such as our addictions, our marriage and family relations problems, depression, anxiety, anger, compulsive perfectionism, dealing with conflict, priorities, and the management of time and money, etc.[40] We need to hold the truths of the gospel in one hand and our unanswered issues in the other. Then we need to work out our understanding of the gospel and its implications via the Scriptures until light breaks through.

We need to apply this same kind of discipline to every area of life. We need to make this our lifestyle.

DEFINING OUR GOALS

The primary goal of spiritual parenting is to see the discipled person rooted and built up in Christ. This is an ongoing process that will continue throughout the person's life. But for this to happen at all, there needs to be a growing understanding of Christ, and of the significance of the things He has done and continues to do. The truths of Christ need to become active agents within us, instructing, correcting, and empowering us.

This need must be very clear in our minds as spiritual parents because it will dictate the kind of nutrition we will provide for our spiritual children. It is so easy to stuff growing Christians with junk food. Junk food can be anything that is not the pure spiritual milk Peter wrote about. It might be taking people through the latest Christian book on the most current topic rather than into the Scriptures. The books might fill their heads with good ideas, but only the Scriptures can fill their hearts with Christ.

How do we lay good foundations? We do it by making Christ our topic, our subject of study. He should be the central figure, the One we are all seeking to know more intimately. Two questions can summarize our agenda and, in fact, our entire Christian experience. They fit the new babe in Christ, and they are just as useful to the person who has followed Christ for forty years. They are the two questions the Apostle Paul asked when he was still "Saul" and Christ knocked him off his horse on the road to Damascus. His two questions were, "Who are you, Lord?" and, "What shall I do, Lord?"[41] We all need to begin the day, every day of our lives, with these two questions, looking to the Scriptures for new answers. We need to go through our days with expectancy as to what He will show us.

In order to lay good foundations, I like to use the Gospels with people who are just starting out. They are four different eye-witness records of Jesus' life and teachings. It is good to imagine, via the narrative in the Gospels, walking the roads with Him, being a part of the audience that heard Him, and watching Him perform His miracles. After going through one of the Gospels, I often take people to the book of Romans. Romans can be tough going and requires study on our part, but there is nothing like that book to help people grasp the significance of the works of Christ and to clarify their understanding of grace by faith.

Then I like to go on to the Epistles. They deal with the out-working of the truths about Christ, their practical implications for everyday life. They are a fertile seed bed for the sprouting of faith, hope, and love.

In summary, our goals for our spiritual offspring are to see them:

- Understand Christ and the truths about Him in such a way that they are secure in their faith, and are being empowered and transformed in all areas of life.
- Develop in faith, hope, and love as an outgrowth of their intimacy with Christ and interdependence in a community.
- Assume their share of the responsibility that is intrinsic to the gospel. That is, that they, as ones who receive this message, begin to participate as message-bearers to the rest of the world.

I can hear the business and management people now. "Those are not *goals*," they object. "They don't meet the criteria of being attainable, observable, and measurable. What kind of performance will you get with goals like these?"

In response, the question has to be, Do you really believe managing by goal setting is compatible with the affairs of the kingdom? There is no doubt that goal setting can greatly increase performance, and that the concept serves us well in areas such as athletics and business. But Jesus said, "My kingdom is not of this world."[42] Can you measure the mustard seed, the yeast in the dough? How do you evaluate an hour spent in prayer? Virtually everything of major importance in God's workings stands outside the reach of our management mechanisms.

The goals I've identified are not measurable, but they are certainly observable. You know when they are present, and you can certainly tell when something is missing. These were the goals Paul had in mind for the first-century Christians who were under his care, and they were certainly not lacking motivation.

QUESTIONS FOR THOUGHT

1. How do you feel about your own foundation in Christ? What has helped you the most in getting it established? What needs do you still have in this area?

2. The author talks about helping people grow in faith, hope and love. In practical terms, how would one proceed to do that?

3. Can you think of an illustration in your life where the truths of the gospel helped you deal with and resolve a difficult issue?

NOTES
1. Galatians 1:6-7.
2. Galatians 4:19.
3. 1 Thessalonians 2:7-11.
4. 1 Peter 2:2-3.
5. 1 John 2:1,18,28.
6. Hebrews 5:11-14.
7. 2 Corinthians 1:24.
8. 1 Corinthians 3:10-11.
9. John 1:29.
10. Hebrews 6:19.
11. Zechariah 3:1-5, Romans 8:31-35, Revelation 12:7-12.
12. Colossians 2:7.

13. 2 Thessalonians 2:1-2.
14. Hebrews 12:2.
15. 1 Peter 1:3.
16. Hebrews 6:19-20.
17. 1 John 3:16.
18. 1 Thessalonians 1:2-3.
19. See Gene Getz, *The Measure of a Church* (Glendale, CA: Regal Books, 1975).
20. Hebrews 12:1-2.
21. 2 Corinthians 8:3.
22. Hebrews 13:9.
23. Ephesians 6:16.
24. Hebrews 10:22.
25. Titus 2:11-14.
26. 2 Corinthians 3:12.
27. Hebrews 6:19.
28. Romans 5:1-2.
29. 1 Corinthians 15:12-22.
30. Philippians 1:20.
31. Matthew 5:44.
32. John 14:23.
33. Ephesians 6:7.
34. Colossians 2:2-3.
35. Matthew 22:34-40; Romans 13:8-10.
36. 2 Corinthians 11:3, NASB.
37. David Powlison, "Integration or Inundation," Colson, Packer, Sproul, *Power Religion* (Chicago, IL: Moody Press, 1992), page 200.
38. Powlison, page 193.
39. Powlison, page 193.
40. Powlison, page 201.
41. Acts 22:8,10.
42. John 18:36.

CHAPTER 4

Spiritual Parents and Growing Children

The more the gospel takes hold of us, the more difficult it becomes to keep quiet about it. When I first began to grow as a Christian the Bible fascinated me, but for some reason the idea of talking to another person about Christ terrified me. I decided to dismiss it. What's wrong with being a silent Christian anyway? I would just enjoy my Bible and let it go at that.

That worked for a while, until I found my mind wandering when I really had to be concentrating. It would always wander to the same subject: the idea of sharing my faith. I wanted to, and I did not want to.

For a few months I managed to dismiss the idea, but finally I had to face it. Where was this notion of sharing my faith coming from? I realized it was because I was beginning to understand the gospel. The desire grew out of the things God was saying to me through the Bible. I either had to put my Bible away or become verbal about my faith. My first attempts were clumsy, embarrassing, and fruitless. I would review the results of each such experience. I didn't want to make the same mistake twice! What did I say? What happened? How should I have done it? What would I say if I could get a replay? Well, things got better, and I'm still learning.

I believe it is a rule that as a Christian grows in his or her understanding of what the Bible is all about and as the Holy Spirit increasingly gains access to the mind, a desire is born that is really from God.

It is a desire that is not much different from the desire a young married couple who are in love experience. They want children. God gives us a similar desire for spiritual children. I have watched this happen in people literally hundreds of times since those days when it first happened to me.

SPIRITUAL PARENTING

Other comparisons can be made between spiritual and physical parenting. In both cases the sense of responsibility can leave one feeling quite inadequate. "What am I going to do with these people? What am I going to give them?" we worry.

When I began trying to help others, I had no idea what I was doing with any of them. I had no plan, and generally speaking we got nowhere. I dreaded the times I was to meet with them, and hoped they wouldn't show up. But when they didn't show I felt devastated. I was desperate for some sense of direction in what I was doing.

This chapter addresses that need. We will describe the stages of growth new believers go through, and discuss the corresponding roles of those who minister to them.

Much has already been written on this subject. This is not new material. The best work I have seen on it was done by Richard Cleveland, Director of the Church Discipleship Ministries for The Navigators. In 1986 he wrote an unpublished paper titled *The Place of Person-to-Person Ministry*. He has given me permission to use this work, and in this section I will be borrowing from it.

STAGES OF GROWTH

The Bible identifies three stages of growth on the road to maturity. Paul refers to the newborn/little child stage,[1] the childhood stage,[2] and the brother/peer stage.[3] The Apostle John identifies the same three stages a bit differently. He talks about children, young men, and fathers.[4] We will refer to these as the newborn/child stage, the youth stage, and the mature brother/sister stage.

The objective is to help a person move from wherever he or she might be to where he or she grows into the full stature of Christ.[5] Of course, we'll never get *there*. One of the greatest gifts God has given us is the infinite opportunity for spiritual growth. But however much we have matured, there is always more beyond. It is in this that we find the adventure of living. There will always be new, unexplored dimensions of His person beckoning to us. The possibilities go off the chart.

What we have said so far can be diagrammed as follows. We'll build on this diagram as we go along to help keep track of what we're saying.

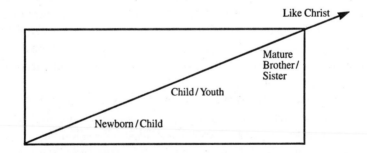

MEETING THE NEEDS OF THE NEWBORN, OR LITTLE CHILD (1 THESSALONIANS 2:7-10)

Paul's purpose for these "children" was that they would experience the benefits of salvation, and demonstrate its fruit. His attitude as he gave himself to moving newborns and children in the faith toward this purpose was that of a mother caring for her little children. He said, "We were gentle among you like a mother caring for her little children."[6] The word translated "caring," according to *Vine's Expository Dictionary*, means "to soften by heat, to keep warm as of birds covering their young with feathers, to cherish with tender love, to foster with tender care."[7]

The image at this stage is of a nurse-mother, tenderly fostering her own children. She is not concerned now to correct every mistake. She doesn't load her children with information. Rather, she is busy making them feel secure in her love and acceptance.

A primary form of instruction at this stage is that of example. In 1 Thessalonians 2:10 Paul relates "how holy, righteous and blameless we were among you." Example is so powerful that it drowns out everything else we say. This is true not just for spiritual infants; it is a rule of life all the way down the line.

If we want our children to learn good table manners, we practice good table manners. If we want them to keep their rooms in order, we keep the rest of the house in order. When they shout at us, we don't shout at them to stop shouting!

If we want new believers to assume the habit of going to the Scriptures daily, we need to be doing it ourselves. If we want them to take their needs to God in prayer, they must see us doing it. Whatever it is that we want new believers to do, we must be doing it ourselves. At the newborn/little child stage, our chief means of influencing is modeling.

The relationship that grows out of this is truly unique. Something special happens that will enrich both you and those you minister to for the rest of your lives. First Thessalonians 2 ends with Paul saying, "Indeed, you are our glory and joy" (verse 20). Ask anyone who has given his or her life to others in this way and he or she will tell you that this is true. Ask anyone about his or her spiritual parent and you will find that that person holds a special place in his or her heart.

The Needs of the Newborn/Little Child
We have seen how two primary needs are protection and love. Together with these, young believers need nourishing—the pure

milk of the word. They need to taste the Lord's goodness,[8] that is, His grace. An understanding of grace is the starting point for all spiritual progress.[9] Grace is an intrinsic part of the foundation we described in the previous chapter. John supports this, saying, "I write to you, dear children, because your sins have been forgiven on account of His name."[10]

The newborn also needs his family. Indeed, everything Paul writes in this passage is directed to the many. The text is in the plural, except where he specifies otherwise. New Christians need individual personal love and a caring community of brothers and sisters. Later in the epistle, Paul writes, "Encourage one another and build each other up, just as in fact you are doing."[11] This community can have many forms, but at this stage it must be characterized by intimacy, safety, and caring.

MEETING THE NEEDS OF THE CHILD, OR YOUTH (1 THESSALONIANS 2:10-12)

The second relationship described in this chapter is that of a father with his children. In this stage, Paul changed both his methods and his objective.

The objective of the nurse-mother could be described as giving her children the heart or desire to grow—a heart for Christ. The objective of the "father" is to equip the child or youth to live a life worthy of God, to live as a citizen of His Kingdom ought to live.

In this stage the young believer needs to learn to assume the responsibility for his own life and ministry. Paul appealed to these young believers to "conduct themselves." It was their responsibility to govern their own behavior. Thus, at this stage people need a little more space, more room to try and fail. And they need a little more responsibility. They need experience.

The approach of the father is described as "encouraging, comforting and urging." According to *Vine's Expository Dictionary*, the word translated "encouraging" means "to call, to beseech, to urge one to pursue some course of conduct."[12] Comfort means "to soothe, console, encourage, stimulating to the earnest discharge of duties."[13] The word translated "urging" means to testify through life and action the worth and effects of faith.[14] Together they defined the expected course of action for the growing believer. He urged them to discipline themselves to "discharge their duties," and he soothed and encouraged them in their attempts.

The Apostle John's observations about "young men" fit perfectly into what we are saying. He says, "I write to you, young men, because you are strong, and the word of God lives in you, and you have overcome the evil one."[15]

Developing the Child/Youth

Many people at this point in their growth could greatly benefit from some consistent, purposeful person-to-person help. The desire is there. A vision for what God could do through them is beginning to bud. They have tried a few things on their own and have discovered how little they know. They are motivated to get a good grasp of the Scriptures so that they can become more fruitfully involved with the people around them.

At this juncture, an invitation to spend extra time together will often be exactly what they're looking for. The purpose for these times needs to be clear. The focus should not be on resolving personal problems. There are other, more effective environments for that. These encounters are for the purpose of equipping the young believer to be effective as an insider. It is to help him or her develop the character and competence necessary to fulfill his or her calling. Personal needs and problems will certainly come up along the way, and they will, of course, need to be attended to. But the relationship should not revolve around problem solving.

Individual personal attention is a very powerful form of ministry. It is also costly. We have only so many hours at our disposal and the tendency, in our attempt to economize time, is to try to do everything through group or congregational forms. If we succumb to that temptation, at the end of the day, that's what we'll have: groups and congregations. But there will be no backbone of strong men and women to give energy and direction to the rest.

MINISTERING WITH BROTHERS AND SISTERS
(1 THESSALONIANS 1:6-10, 2:13-16)

The third way Paul related to the Thessalonian Christians was as a brother. In the nurse-mother stage his purpose was to see them grow in a healthy manner, enthusiastic about the things they were experiencing through their faith. In the brother/sister stage he was endeavoring to get them to live as mature Christians who were assuming the responsibility for their own Christian life and ministry. This third stage is marked by evidences that they have indeed embraced both the message and the task. They have gotten on board with Paul to work together for the growth of the gospel.

He commended them because they had "received the word . . . as it actually is, the word of God, which is at work in you."[16] Then he went on to commend them for their faithfulness in the midst of persecution for the sake of the gospel. They embraced the *message* and they embraced the *task*.

Paul treated these people as his peers. He saw them as standing shoulder to shoulder with him. Because of their maturity he felt free to move on and leave it all to them. Not that he would ever forget them or that they would ever forget him. He never stopped praying for them and he kept in touch through letters, personal visits, and the visits of special gifted co-laborers, but he moved on.

To summarize the things we have just said, let's revisit the earlier diagram and make some additions.

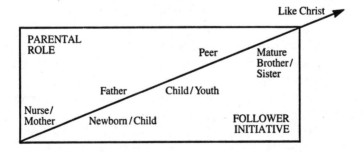

It is important to observe the changing role of the spiritual parent as the young Christian matures. It goes from the casual but attentive role of the mother to a more deliberate father role. This second role requires a more spacious environment. Finally, parent and offspring are relating and working together as peers.

This process I have described may sound complicated, beyond reach and hopelessly time consuming. We will talk about how to find the time in chapter 13. For now, let's stick to the process. It is really not that difficult.

STAYING ON TRACK

I find I need to periodically step back from what I'm doing with people to stop and reflect. I need to regain my understanding of the situation of each person. I do this by setting aside a day about every six months to get alone to pray and think. I get out of the house and away from the office and head for a favorite spot at the top of a hill.

I begin by praying for the people I feel God has brought into my life. As I pray, I attempt to discern what each one needs that I can perhaps provide. I write my thoughts down. I ask four basic questions:

1. *Where is this person now in his or her walk with Christ?* What progress has the person made? What gifts and abilities are becoming evident?
2. *What is he or she ready for?* Jesus said, "I have much more to say to you, more than you can now bear."[17] We need to be sensitive to timing, to readiness according to their needs, not any agenda of ours.
3. *What is most urgent?* Some problems or needs can wait. Others cannot. Wisdom is knowing which are which. What, I ask, will most help the person go on to the next level of maturity, or break a logjam and get him or her moving again?
4. *How can I help?* This one takes a bit of prayerful creativity. Perhaps the person needs to be thrown into a

sink-or-swim responsibility. Perhaps it's the opposite: He might need to be rescued! Perhaps the need is for more time together, or to make plans to get a mutual unbelieving friend into the Scriptures with us.

I've found that God faithfully guides me into answers to these questions as I spend this extended time in prayer. I then proceed over the next months on the basis of the orientation I get on these occasions.

SPIRITUALITY, SPIRITUAL MATURITY—AND TIME

We need to add one more factor to our diagram. It is time.

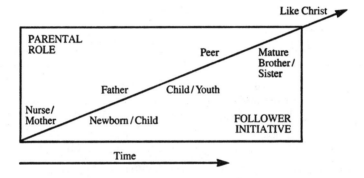

What kind of time are we talking about? How long does it take for a person to grow from spiritual birth to adulthood: a year, two years, five?

An American student worker once explained to me how they worked on a one-year time frame, to correspond with the academic year. He said they needed to major on evangelism in the fall so that they could have their converts by the end of October. That way, they could get people through the Bible study books by spring so that they would be spiritually mature enough to make it through summer vacation. He was obviously operating on his own agenda for the people he ministered to. That was before the spiritual ice age hit the campuses.

How long it takes for people to reach maturity depends upon where they're starting from and the kinds of problems they're living with as they come into the Family. Recently one of the pastors of a large church that is attracting boomers, who are migrating back in, told me it takes a full year of teaching in their new members class to bring these people to where they understand the gospel enough so that they can respond to it. After all, their heritage is gone and so they must start at the beginning. It takes much longer than you may think at first.

So, if your agenda has time tables on it, throw it away. This is especially critical for people we reach as insiders. I have found that it can often take a decade for a person to decide to follow Christ, to manage to overcome the major problems in his or her life, and then, finally, to begin to bear fruit in the lives of the people around him or her. "Oaks of righteousness" do not grow up overnight.

We often make a mistake in this area that causes confusion and does damage to people. I have seen immature Christians, because of their spirituality, put into positions of responsibility they couldn't possibly maintain. They fail to carry the load and then spend the rest of their lives picking up the pieces.

Many times brand-new believers seem to undergo a total transformation from one day to another. They are delivered from their addictions, their lives are filled with new joy, and they boldly tell everyone within earshot about what Christ has done for them. I would not question whether or not this experience is of the Spirit of God. A brand-new believer can and should be spiritual. But a new believer cannot be mature. Maturity comes only with time.

Spirituality is living in dependence on the Spirit of God, and even a new believer—one who has yet to learn there are two testaments in the Bible—can do that. Spirituality is a matter of humility before God and faith in Christ. But there is more to our walk with God than this. As time goes on, if we do not fuel our faith with an increasing understanding of Christ, it will weaken—and we will not mature.

Immature people are vulnerable. They can be blown about by any kind of teaching that comes along.[18] So our joyful, intrepid day-old believer has not suddenly come into perpetual bliss. There will be plenty of hard times ahead. We need to understand that and expect it.

Spirituality and maturity are distinct from each other, yet they are interdependent. To be spiritual is to be dependent on the Holy Spirit. This dependence should characterize our normal, everyday relationship with Him. The fruit of this relationship is love, joy, peace, patience, gentleness, goodness, and self-control.[19]

Maturity comes in time, out of a spiritual life that is nourished by an increasing knowledge of Christ through experiences with Him. Its fruit is intimacy with Christ, Christlike character, perseverance, and power.[20]

WHEN THINGS GO WRONG

As I began to write this book, some people who heard about it wrote to urge me to address some of the abuses that happen under the guise of discipleship. One person wrote, "I have never really forgiven my apartment leader for the controlling and emotionally damaging way in which she 'discipled' us. I'm dealing with this now."

Another person sent me a copy of a master's thesis on obsessive-compulsive personality disorders. His paper shows how the discipler-disciple relationship can fit into an obsessive-compulsive pattern, as one person exercises inordinate control over another. Over time such an approach generates inner resentments within the dependent personality that often never go away.

I have seen this happen. I have also attended to my share of victims. The process of controlling another person follows a pattern. It happens when an authoritarian person establishes a set of goals of accomplishment and productivity that are later used as measurements. These performance standards determine acceptance or rejection, approval or disapproval. Usually the goals and standards themselves are arbitrarily chosen. They are reflections of the personality of the authoritarian leader, of his or her personal preferences, rather than biblical standards. But even biblical truth can be abused in the same manner. The message that was intended to bring freedom can cause bondage when misapplied.[21]

In the previous chapter we talked about setting our compass on True North. The kind of abuse we're talking about here is an example of what can happen when we use any "compass bearing" other than Christ. Our false "North" can be an authoritarian person. It can be a vision, a task, an organization, a local church—or self-fulfillment. All of these are common, all are a form of idolatry, and they all lead to bondage and disillusionment.

So something like this could happen to our diagram. There are casualties:

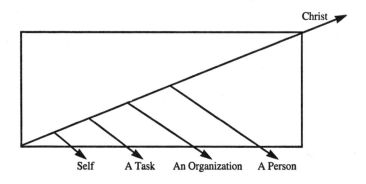

Christ

Self   A Task   An Organization   A Person

SETTING OUR COMPASS

> Let us throw off everything that hinders and the sin that so
> easily entangles, and let us run with perseverance the race
> marked out for us. Let us fix our eyes on Jesus.[22]

We have just seen what can happen when we are not focused on Christ. There is only one way to go to reach maturity. It is interesting that this Scripture passage also says there is a course, really a trajectory, marked out for us. We are to follow a certain route. There are three tracks on it.

Nobody arrives at maturity on his own. He needs his brothers and sisters. They need to serve him and he needs to serve them. So we arrive at maturity via *community*. Then there are things that must be learned along the way. There are truths we need to understand and certain skills we must acquire if we are to know Him and be faithful servants. We need *competence* to get down the road to maturity.

One more thing is required, perhaps the most important of all, and the most difficult to come by. It is *character*. Character is what you are. It's what you are *in the dark*—for better or worse. Godly character keeps on keeping on. It will get you there.

So, with our compasses set on Christ and with these three tracks to follow, we have charted our course. These tracks will be prominent in our discussions through the rest of the book.

QUESTIONS FOR THOUGHT

In this chapter we have divided the stages of growth toward maturity into three parts: the newborn/child, the youth, and the mature brother or sister. Reflect back on what you read and then identify the two or three needs you feel are most critical in each of these stages.

1. The newborn/child.
2. The youth.
3. Mature brothers and sisters.

By what means (people, activities, etc.) do you think each of these needs could be met?

NOTES
1. 1 Thessalonians 2:7.
2. 1 Thessalonians 2:11.
3. 1 Thessalonians 2:14.
4. 1 John 2:12-14.
5. Ephesians 4:13.
6. 1 Thessalonians 2:7.
7. W.E. Vine, *Vine's Expository Dictionary of Old and New Testament Words*, vol. 1 (Old Tappan, NJ: Fleming H. Revell, 1981), page 184.
8. 1 Peter 2:2-3.
9. Colossians 1:6.
10. 1 John 2:12.

11. 1 Thessalonians 5:11.
12. Vine, vol. 2, page 60.
13. Vine, vol. 1, page 208.
14. Vine, vol. 4, page 225.
15. 1 John 2:14.
16. 1 Thessalonians 2:13.
17. John 16:12.
18. Ephesians 4:14.
19. Galatians 5:22-23.
20. Ephesians 3:16-20.
21. Galatians 5:1.
22. Hebrews 12:1-2.

CHAPTER 5

New Creations in Christ

"The old has gone, the new has come!"[1]

T he first goal of spiritual growth is for a person to be founded in Christ. The next is to be built up in Him. The evidence that this building is going on will be the presence of faith, hope, and love—together with the attending virtues that these three generate. The ultimate goal is to become like Christ. This is maturity. We should be growing in His direction all our lives. We discussed all this in chapter 3.

Chapter 4 gave us an overview of the growth process. We identified the stages of spiritual growth and the kinds of care, or attention, a person needs at each stage along the way.

The purpose of this book is to help equip the insider to be faithful in enabling others to know Christ and grow in Him. We will develop this topic over the next several chapters. To be competent in discipling others, we need a thorough understanding of the dynamics of the growth process. This means we will need to explore questions such as, What is "conversion"? What happens at that point? What doesn't happen? What kind of help can a new believer expect from God? What kinds of struggles can he anticipate? How should he handle suffering or adversity? How should they be interpreted? What is a proper response? We will be addressing these questions in the next chapters.

In this chapter we will start at the beginning of spiritual life: at conversion. Our purpose is to understand what it is, how it occurs, what changes take place at that point—and what doesn't change.

CONVERSION INCLUDES RECEIVING
GOD'S RIGHTEOUSNESS

Justice and righteousness—a refrain that runs from Genesis through Revelation. Over and over the Scriptures use this phrase to describe an attribute of God. Actually it is a single Greek word in the New Testament: *dikaiosune*. The words "justice" and "righteousness" appear in the Old Testament alone over one hundred times. This is one of those concepts so rich in meaning it requires a paragraph to define it. It was formerly translated "rightwiseness," which, even though it is not in our dictionary, communicates!

Other terms that help fill out the meaning are faithfulness, truthfulness, righteousness, and holiness, which are expressed in the condemnation of sin. There is also the concept of judicial righteousness, of God's rule as King and Judge.[2]

It would be a profitable investment to read your Bible through and underline the words justice and righteousness every time they appear. You would come out of it with a deepened understanding of God and His ways.

Justice and righteousness define the nature of God's rule. For example, Isaiah wrote concerning Christ,

> He will not judge by what he sees with his eyes,
>   or decide by what he hears with his ears;
> but with righteousness he will judge the needy,
>   with justice he will give decisions for the poor of
>   the earth.[3]

The most immediate observation on this passage is that God's perspective on justice and righteousness runs far deeper than our own. Our equipment is too limited. All we have at our disposal by which to judge are our eyes and ears. So we say, "He did it! I saw him with my own eyes." Or, "She said it! I heard her with my own ears." That's enough to win your case in court.

But Christ will not judge by what He sees or hears. *Instead*, He will judge with justice and righteousness. Given our limited equipment in contrast to His, we should retire from the field.

Yet we judge. The one we judge most often is God Himself! Have you ever considered how strange it is that God's most frequent claim about Himself is that He is righteous and just, while our most frequent complaint against Him is that He is unjust? We go through a crisis or suffer a tragedy, and the first words on our lips are, "Why did God allow this to happen?"

The question is really an accusation. With it, we are filing a complaint against Him. We make a great step forward in our growth when we, in our hearts, abandon such complaints and relax in His "rightwiseness."

Given the constant referral to God's righteousness and justice in the Old Testament, it is no surprise that Jesus would focus on the same theme. He came proclaiming the good news of the Kingdom, and that, in itself, speaks to the subject. "Righteousness and justice are the foundation of his throne."[4] If that is what His Kingdom is all about, then only the righteous can have any part in it.

In Matthew 5 Jesus made this point in a way that no one who was there that day would ever forget. A multitude of people were gathered around Jesus and He was talking to them. The Pharisees and teachers of the Law were there, nursing their grave reservations about Jesus. The subject, as usual, was the Kingdom of God, which the people didn't understand then any better than we do now.

Jesus said, "Unless your *righteousness* surpasses that of the Pharisees and the teachers of the law, you will certainly not enter the kingdom of heaven."[5]

Now the scribes were professional students of religion and

the Pharisees were those who lived according to their teachings. Both were motivated by the sole concern of achieving righteousness. They worked hard at it. They had carefully defined the 613 laws of Moses, and had clarified what it meant to keep or break each one. They fasted weekly, prayed out loud on the streets several times a day, tithed, and wore Bible verses etched in leather on their foreheads. The rest of the populace lived in awe of such piety.

Imagine the public reaction to Jesus' statement that to enter the Kingdom of Heaven a person would have to do better, be more righteous than the Pharisees and scribes. Everybody had to be ready to give up. "If even the scribes aren't going to make it," they must have thought, "what hope is there for us? We have to work for a living."

That was the reaction Jesus was after. He had made His point.

What was the point? The Apostle Paul makes it clear in his letter to the Romans. He writes, "For I can testify about them that they are zealous for God, but their zeal is not based on knowledge. Since they did not know the *righteousness* that comes from God and sought to establish their own, they did not submit to God's *righteousness*. Christ is the end of the law so that there may be *righteousness* for everyone who believes."6

The point is, even if we spent twenty-four hours a day working at being righteous, that wouldn't be good enough. No one ever got anywhere on the basis of their own righteousness. A person must receive Christ's righteousness, "And be found in him, not having a *righteousness* of my own that comes from the law, but that which comes through faith in Christ—the *righteousness* that comes from God through faith."7 As God looks at us, the question is not, Am I good enough? It is, Was Christ good enough? It is not, Is God pleased with my work? It is, Is He pleased with Christ's work?

Everything we saw in chapter 3, the great truths of the incarnation, the sacrifice, the resurrection, and ascension, converge to make this gift of righteousness available to us through God's grace.

An understanding of grace is the starting point for all spiritual progress. "All over the world," Paul writes, "this gospel is bearing fruit and growing, just as it has been doing among you since the day you heard it and *understood God's grace in all its truth*."[8]

This is a very difficult truth for new believers to grasp. They have it, and then they don't. They see it, and then it slips out of focus. The difficulty with God's grace is that it's just too good to be true. Surely, we reason, my good behavior, or my bad behavior, has some influence on my standing with God. But it doesn't!

When we give up our rebellion and receive Christ's righteousness, we are fit for the Kingdom of God. That is conversion.

WHAT HAPPENS AT CONVERSION?

At conversion a new believer will often experience a euphoria that results in totally unrealistic expectations of what life is going to be like from that point on. Someone shows him the verse, "If anyone is in Christ, he is a new creation."[9] He takes that to mean he has been permanently and completely transformed. He has set himself up for disillusionment.

The first time I met Mike he had been a Christian for a week. His life to that point had been very difficult. He had been at war with both his father and his employer. He had become so desperate that he had come close to ending it all by crashing his plane into the control tower of the local airport where his employer worked.

But now, he told me, all of that was gone. The hatred and despair had vanished, replaced by love for Christ and a new zest for life.

I had looked Mike up because he had asked to talk to me. He had decided God was calling him to go to China as a missionary, and he had heard that I could help him get there.

I tried to encourage him to slow down and spend some time growing, but he was resolute. He was convinced that he was ready and that the Holy Spirit would compensate for anything he lacked as he went along.

Mike was obviously setting himself up for major disillusionment. The conversation lengthened into hours. He finally agreed to make an intermediate stop to reside, for a period, in the city where I was living. I promised to help him mature in his Christian life.

A few weeks later Mike arrived in our city. We helped him move into a house where three other Christians were living, and helped him find a job.

It didn't take long for a new set of conflicts to develop around Mike. He had trouble with his new employer, and he was finding some of his roommates hard to live with. In time, Mike became so discouraged he contemplated finding another control tower to crash his plane into.

Today Mike is a mature, faithful believer with a solid marriage and family. But he is one of those people who needed a decade to get the pieces together.

What happened here? Why didn't that first flush of joy continue? Why did most of his old problems return? Why did it take him so long to really overcome them? These are very important questions. It is essential that we understand what takes place at conversion, and what *doesn't* take place—what *does* change and what *doesn't*. Realistic, biblical answers to these questions can enable us to protect new believers from disillusionment and give them a basis for solid spiritual growth.

What Does Change?

Profound, eternal changes occur at the time of conversion. Some of them have to do with our status, or position. Others alter our immediate condition.

Changes in Status

As for you, you were dead. . . . You followed the ways of this world and of the ruler of the kingdom of the air. . . . But . . . God . . . made us alive with Christ . . . raised us up with Christ and seated us with him in the heavenly realms. . . . Consequently, you are no longer foreigners and aliens, but fellow citizens with God's people and members of God's household. . . . You too are being built together to become a dwelling in which God lives by his Spirit.[10]

This passage describes well the changes that take place in our status when we become believers, and there are many other passages. They have to do with our relationships, our destiny, and our identity. Conversion changes who we are. It also changes the status of our relationship to sin. We're paid up—no longer in debt to sin.

In time, as we mature, these changes in our status have increasing influence on the way we live life. As we comprehend the magnitude of God's generosity toward us, we begin to live according to our new identity.

But these changes in status won't do much for the new believer when his violent temper has just exploded on his wife—again. He needs immediate first aid!

Changes in Circumstances—When we respond to God's love and submit to Him, He responds to us by giving us the gift of the Holy Spirit, who is capable of giving first aid—and a lot more.

His intention in coming to live in us is to empower us. But He will not do anything against our wills. A Christian could be described as someone in whom two persons dwell. In fact, our spiritual life or spiritual death is determined by whether the Holy Spirit is in us or not. "If anyone does not have the Spirit of Christ, he does not belong to Christ."[11]

I wonder if it's possible for a person to have the Holy Spirit residing in his or her life and be unaffected by Him. The One who created the universe is bound to cause a stir as He begins doing His creative work in our lives. As He creates a new nature in us, we will experience new desires, new values, and new attitudes. There will be a hunger to know God better and a desire to be around brothers and sisters in our new family. He changes our relationship to sin. It will not look as attractive as it did before. We'll still sin, but not like we used to. And when we do, we'll hate it afterward.

The Holy Spirit comes to serves as our counselor and teacher.[12] He gives us wisdom and empowers us.[13] He gives us gifts so that we can serve God by serving others.[14] He helps us pray. To have the Holy Spirit is to have everything we could possibly need.[15]

So what's new? Many things. We have a new status, a new identity. We have the Holy Spirit living in us, and a new nature.

What Doesn't Change?

Unfortunately we are going to have to wait until we join Christ to complete our transformation.[16] Our brain cells don't change at conversion. We still have the same old bodies, the same temperaments, psychological characteristics, and personalities. Our storehouse of memories is distressingly intact, and the same old behavioral and emotional patterns continue to run their familiar course.

We are a mixed bag, a mixture of good and bad. But the Holy Spirit wants to help us change it all. He wants to enhance and redirect what is good and He wants to break up the bad, destructive patterns. Our old nature is going to put up resistance against that. Therein lies the conflict that is inherent to the Christian life.

Civil War

The two passages of Scripture that describe most completely this conflict between the old and the new natures are Romans 6–8 and Galatians 5. Galatians 5:17 summarizes, "For the sinful nature desires what is contrary to the Spirit, and the Spirit what is contrary to the sinful nature. They are in conflict with each other, so that you do not do what you want."

Romans 8:5-8 cuts to the heart of the matter. This passage teaches us that the battleground of this civil war is the mind. Our sinful nature wants its way in our minds, but the Holy Spirit also wants to be our instructor. That makes sense, since the mind is the control room for all of life. The sinful nature has a distinct advantage. It has the seniority. It has had exclusive control over our minds all our lives. It knows its way around in it. We are accustomed to its ways. The Holy Spirit is the newcomer.

There is a strong natural attraction to what the sinful nature offers as it bargains for control over us. It plays to our sensuality, our appetites. It says, "Gratify your cravings, follow your desires and thoughts."[17] Sounds attractive, doesn't it?

The Holy Spirit makes a different offer. He warns us, "Don't listen to the sinful nature. Satan is its master. It offers a moment of pleasure at the expense of a lifetime of pain—and then death. It will cause you to self-destruct. Set your minds on what I desire for you. The fruit of doing things My way is life and peace."

It's a tough choice, sometimes. There will be conflict and war—with casualties.

The spiritual parent is absolutely crucial to this struggle. Many times just his or her presence is enough to decide the issue. Prayer—intercession—is another deciding factor. Also, the spiritual parent knows that one way or another, the new believer needs to reinforce the Holy Spirit's position in the mind by filling it with God's thoughts. That's what the Bible is: God's thoughts in print. God's thoughts should predominate in all our minds all the time.

That in itself goes a long way in determining the tide of the battle.

There is much more to this matter of spiritual transformation, as we shall see in the following chapters.

QUESTIONS FOR THOUGHT

1. How should we respond when a new Christian crashes and seems to revert back to his or her old ways?

2. What things can the spiritual parent do to strengthen the new believer? What are the limits to what he or she can do? What are some things that only the Holy Spirit can do?

3. What part should community play in these early stages of a believer's walk with God?

NOTES

1. 2 Corinthians 5:17.
2. *a.* Gerhard Kittle, *Theological Dictionary of the New Testament*, vol. II (Grand Rapids, MI: Eerdmans Publishing Co., 1964), page 195. *b.* W.E. Vine, *Vine's Expository Dictionary of Old and New Testament Words*, vol. 3 (Old Tappan, NJ: Fleming H. Revell, 1971), page 298.
3. Isaiah 11:3-4.
4. Psalm 97:2.
5. Matthew 5:20.
6. Romans 10:2-4.
7. Philippians 3:9-10.
8. Colossians 1:6.
9. 2 Corinthians 5:17.
10. Ephesians 2:1-2,4-6,19,22.
11. Romans 8:9.
12. John 14:15-17.
13. Ephesians 3:14-21.
14. 1 Corinthians 12:7-11.
15. Galatians 5:22-23.
16. 1 John 3:2.
17. Ephesians 2:3.

CHAPTER 6

True Spiritual Transformation

I n order to get a realistic understanding of what happens at conversion, we looked at the changes occurring at that initial encounter. It is evident that inner conflict breaks out as the new nature we received from the Holy Spirit begins to lay claim to territory that had, until then, been the undisputed domain of the sinful nature. Becoming a Christian means signing on for a lifetime of change. Many of these changes will be accompanied by great struggle. War will break out at times as the old, sinful nature and the new nature battle it out over a particular issue.

That really doesn't sound all that interesting, you say. Isn't there any other way to do this? Is there a Plan B? There is a Plan B and, in fact, that is where many people live. Let's put it into visual form.

Before conversion, we went our own way, following our own desires. "You followed the ways of the world and of the ruler of the kingdom of the air. . . . All of us lived at one time gratifying the cravings of our sinful nature."[1] We were headed in the opposite direction from God.

God ⟶ The Unbeliever

Then God reaches out to us with His message. It stops us. We respond to it. The essential response is repentance. Repentance is a change of mind that involves both a turning from sin and a turning to God.[2] So conversion means an about-face.[3]

Conversion

God

Plan B is simply to stop, turn—and go no further! The person will make some adjustment, give up a few habits, quit saying "damn," and join the church. But other than that, it's pretty much life as usual. I don't believe it's possible to deliberately enter into a relationship with Christ with Plan B in mind. The terms of conversion don't allow for it. But many people, after making a decision for Christ, for one reason or another don't go much further.

I have a friend who is a pastor. He was in a very large church and enjoyed great popularity. He's a very gifted Bible expositor, and several times every Sunday the church building would fill with people just to listen to him.

One day as we were having breakfast together, he confided in me that he was leaving the church and moving to another part of the country to take a church in a city that is known for its spiritual indifference. I expressed surprise. So he explained, "Preaching in this town full of churches is like trying to punch your way out of a marshmallow. I give it everything I've got, but I'm getting nowhere with these people. Nothing ever changes!" He was moving to a part of the country where people don't believe, *and know they don't.*

Churches are full of people who are on Plan B, and it's killing the church.

Also, Plan B is a frightening place to be in. A person who is in this category needs to question the very validity of his or her experience with God. The story of the event may be clear in the person's mind: "It was at summer Bible camp back in 1978. We had a bonfire, I realized. . . . And I remember feeling so good afterward."

To that, the Apostle Paul would say, "Examine yourselves to see whether you are in the faith; test yourselves. Do you not realize that Christ Jesus is in you—unless, of course, you fail the test?"[4] You can think you're on Plan B when, in fact, you never really made the turn at all.

Another downside to Plan B, assuming you are in fact a Christian, is that whatever faith you might have is really quite useless. It is useless to you and it is useless to God. Your life will be affected by the same consequences you would suffer if you did not have Christ at all. As for your usefulness to God, "If a man cleanses himself" the Bible says, "he will be an instrument for noble purposes, made holy, useful to the Master and prepared to do any good work."[5] God is going to reach for a cleaner vessel than you to do His work.

To live by Plan B is, in the *best* case, to live a useless life. The person that is on Plan A is geared toward responding to God for the rest of his or her life. His life looks like this:

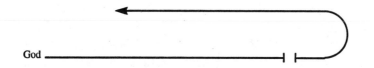

God

In this chapter we want to explore the nature of true spiritual transformation. The changes God is interested in producing in us go far deeper than merely dropping some old behavior patterns and replacing them with new ones. His intention is to *remake* us! "We are God's workmanship, created in Christ Jesus."[6] The word translated "workmanship" means "something produced by an artisan."[7] God is the artisan. If we let Him, He will create out of each of us an original piece of art. The verse communicates the idea that He will be constantly tinkering with us, shaping us, until He gets us just right. This will go on throughout our entire life span.

There is a diagram anthropologists use as a descriptive device to study a people. It separates out certain elements of a culture. This enables them to study each part by itself. Then, by observing the interaction between the elements, the culture under study begins to make sense.

I have found it helpful to use this same diagram to communicate the kind of transformation that needs to occur as we become a new creation in Christ. We will use just three elements in our diagram: world view, values, and behavior.

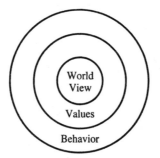

Everyone has a *world view*. It is made up of the person's answers to the big questions of existence. How do I understand the universe, its origins? What about the natural world? How did it come about? Why did it come about? What about me? What am I? Why do I exist? What is my notion of God, or gods?

A person's answers to these questions will determine how he or she approaches life. Even if a person writes in "I don't know" to all the questions, the effect will be the same. Not knowing, agnosticism, is then the controlling philosophy. My world view tells me who I am.

A person's world view will determine his *values*. Values are those things that are of such importance to a person that they motivate his or her behavior. If, for example, I believe I am nothing more than a biological accident, that I, together with the natural world, just happened, that belief will be reflected in the things I attach importance to. Self-fulfillment would certainly be close to the top of the list.

Behavior reflects our world view plus our values. It acts out how we perceive ourselves and what we consider to be important. So if self-fulfillment is a driving value, my behavior will tend in that direction. I will spend a lot of my time and energy pursuing the things that make me feel good about myself.

So world view, values, and behavior serve as a basic framework for understanding ourselves. This illustration is an oversimplification of the human experience and breaks down if we try to use it to explain everything. It is limited in several ways. For one, there are other sources of behavior that didn't make it into this diagram. You'll see what I mean when we get into the next chapter.

But this diagram is useful in helping us understand where, at what levels, change needs to occur if there is to be true transformation. If we don't read more than this into it, we will be okay.

TRANSFORMATION FROM WITHIN

Where must change take place? One look at the diagram and the answer is obvious. Change must occur at the core, in our world view, in the things we believe. If things change there, values will follow in time, and behavior will not be far behind. Transformation comes from within, and works its way on out. Conversion lays the foundation for changes in our world view.

An understanding of the interplay between world view, values, and behavior helps us know how to minister to others. If we want to see true transformation occur, our efforts should be oriented toward affecting what a person believes and values. That helps us take wrong behavior in stride. We know that in time genuine changes in behavior will appear.

It is interesting to note that this sequence of world view, values, and behavior could serve as the outline for several of the Epistles Paul wrote to the churches, particularly Ephesians,

Philippians, and Colossians. They begin with the big picture. They focus on Christ and His purposes. Then they move to the implications of that picture. Finally, they get very specific on matters of behavior. Let me illustrate with the book of Ephesians.

Paul begins the letter talking about God's grand, eternal purposes. Then he places us in the middle of those purposes, and goes to work on the subject of our identity. We are seated with Christ as members of God's household, he tells us. We are citizens of God's Kingdom, and so on. Anyone who will invest the effort to understand this book of Ephesians will be rewarded with a very robust sense of identity. It gives us a biblical *world view*.

Then Paul moves to the implications. If this is what is going on, and if this is who you are, he says, then certain things assume primary importance. Knowing Christ better, suffering with Him, being filled with Him, unity with God's people, and growing to spiritual maturity will become your priorities. These are *values*. They are the things that are of such importance that they motivate us to action.

Paul then moves on to application. He goes into the various ideas of *behavior*. But notice how each exhortation is framed. He says,

Live a life of love, *just as Christ loved us.*[8]

Submit to one another *out of reverence for Christ.*[9]

Wives, submit to your husbands *as to the Lord.*[10]

Husbands, love your wives, *just as Christ loved.*[11]

Children, obey your parents *in the Lord.*[12]

Slaves, obey . . . *just as you would obey Christ.*

—and so on.

There must be cause and effect between truth and behavior. Paul shows why the behavior he calls for is reasonable. It is reasonable because of the things we know about Christ and because of who we have become in His hands. This lifts behavior up from being a dutiful adherence to the letter of the law to where it becomes a celebration of love for the One who has loved us so profoundly.

GETTING IT ALL BACKWARDS

So often, as we attempt to help others in the Christian life, we get these things turned around. We focus on behavior rather than on the transformation of the heart. We say, "So you want to follow Christ! Very well. Here are some things you must do. And over here we have another list of things you would do well to give up." And we give them the two lists.

My colleague Ken Lottis pointed out that when we do this, when we put the emphasis on behavior rather than on the inner person, all we are doing is changing the label on the same old can. Our diagram looks like this:

We may get someone to look like a Christian for a while that way, but he or she will be headed for trouble. Discipling that is performance-oriented will often eventually lead to either rebellion or bondage.

INSTITUTIONALIZING OUR SPIRITUAL CHILDREN

Another effect of modernization is institutionalization. Institutions existed long before modernization began, but we have made institutionalization our way of life. We live in an institutionalized society and spend our lives relating to a broad set of its codes. We have the institutions of our government; we have military institutions; institutions of education, health, and business. We also have our religious institutions.

We couldn't live in a complex society like ours without institutions. We would all go mad. Institutions are to the society what personal habits are to an individual. In our personal lives, we have turned over to habit at least ninety percent of what we do. These habits range from the time and manner in which we get up in the morning, to the "getting ready for work" ritual, to what we do first at the office, and on through the day. Personal habits free up our minds to think about more important matters. They run the routine part of our lives.

Institutions, the way I'm using the term here, are organizations that have established a set of laws, policies, customs, practices, and systems. These procedures become self-sustaining. A self-sustaining system is called a bureaucracy. A bureaucracy is a subdivision or department within an institution that is managed through following inflexible routines.[13]

When applied to matters of spiritual growth, this "hardening of the routines" can destroy the health of any Christian. When a new believer comes to Christ, we tell him he is getting into a personal relationship with Christ, and then we promptly put him into a program. The church mirrors the ways of our society. The government gets its work done through bureaucracies. We get ours done through programs. There are several problems inherent in this, but the one we're concerned about here is the message this communicates to the new Christian about the nature of the Christian life.

Our turning everything into systems or programs imposes conformity. To belong, the person must be a part of the program. The program imposes a certain conformity of behavior. When this pressure to conform becomes the overriding influence, the matters that really count—those that produce true spiritual transformation—are lost. It is very easy to confuse "doing the program" with being a Christian. The two can become equated in a person's mind. There are several examples of this in the New Testament.

The most dramatic example is found in Paul's letter to the Galatians. These people were the fruit of the first missionary journey of Paul and Barnabas. They had come to Christ out of paganism. They had been worshipers of the gods of the cosmic elements, the stars, fire, and so on. The New Testament Greek word for these elements is *stoicheia*, translated "the basic principles of the world."[14]

Paul reminded the Galatians how bad life had been for them before they had come into Christ. It was a kind of slavery. Pagan religions *do* enslave. The powers of the gods of the sun, wind, and stars were terrifying, trapping people in superstition and fear.

Then Paul warned the Galatians that they were heading back into the same kind of slavery. He asked, "Now that you know God—or rather are known by God—how is it that you are turning back to those *weak and miserable principles?*" This is his second use of the word *stoicheia*.

Now this is very interesting! The Galatians weren't getting out their old gods, Zeus, Aries and the lot. They weren't reverting to their old cultic practices. They were headed in an opposite direction. They were picking up some of the Jewish tradition. Some were beginning to observe Jewish feast and fast days. They were switching to kosher foods and getting circumcised. Certainly mixing a little Judaism with one's faith in Christ couldn't be as bad as sacrificing a chicken to the stars. But according to Paul it was all the same. Any system of human origin, whether the pagan or the Jewish system, is *stoicheia*.

The word *stoicheia* appears two more times in the New Testament, both in the letter to the Colossians. Paul uses it in 2:8 and in 2:20-23. Here he carries his same point one step further. He asks, "Since you died with Christ to the basic principles of this world (*stoicheia*), why, as though you still belonged to it, do you submit to its rules: 'Do not handle! Do not taste! Do not touch?' These are all destined to perish . . . because they are based on human commands and teachings. Such regulations indeed have an appearance of wisdom . . . but they lack any value in restraining sensual indulgence."[15]

Sensual indulgence is, of course, the real issue. What he's saying is that rules and regulations will not solve your problem of sensual behavior. The solutions must run at a deeper level. The way to deal with sensual indulgence, Paul goes on to say, is to "set your hearts on things above, where Christ is seated. . . . Set your minds on things above."[16] This is what we've been talking about in this chapter: changing your world view.

CONCLUSION

When people come to Christ, they step into the light, out of the darkness. During those years of groping around in the dark, a lot goes wrong. All this wrong comes to light in the presence of Christ.[17] We as spiritual parents begin to see what's there: the moral compromises, the unlawful business practices, the live-in girlfriend, and so on. They are the grave clothes from the years of living in death. Our first impulse is to send the person to the showers and give him a new set of clothes. We would feel more comfortable around the person if he were cleaned up just a bit.

But whose job is it to make those changes? We have a part, yes—but God must do the work. Our part is to accept the person, while exposing him or her to the truth of God's Word. Over time the grave clothes will come off, being replaced by "rich garments."[18]

It requires faith and patience for us to do things this way. "What if he doesn't stop living with his girlfriend?" we worry. "What if he doesn't figure out that a certain practice needs to change? When should I step in?" I have found I seldom have to say much—as long as we are going to the Scriptures together. Some bad habits take longer to break than others, and some good habits take longer to acquire than others, but the change eventually comes if the person is serious about following Christ. When changes occur in this fashion, the outcome is freedom rather than bondage.

The alternative approach carries a lot of risk with it. When we begin by giving a young Christian our personal version of the rules, when that is the first thing he or she gets from us, we might get that person's conformity—but it won't be out of conviction. So it will be done in the flesh, by willpower rather than by the Spirit's power. This fosters two misconceptions: The first is, "God will accept me if I obey these rules and reject me if I don't." The second is, "It's up to me to make this Christian life work." Grace is obscured in either case.

QUESTIONS FOR THOUGHT

1. Ask yourself two basic questions about your world view and values:

   How would you fill in the center circle? Who are you? Why are you here? How would you describe God?

   What would you say are the four or five major values that motivate your life? What is of greatest importance to you?

2. Reflect on your answers to question 1. Do you see correlations between the things you've said and the way you live life, your behavior?

3. What does this tell you about bringing about change in your own life?

NOTES
1. Ephesians 2:1-3.
2. W. E. Vine, *Vine's Expository Dictionary of Old and New Testament Words*, vol. 1 (Old Tappan, NJ: Fleming H. Revell, 1981), page 281.
3. Acts 20:21.
4. 2 Corinthians 13:5.
5. 2 Timothy 2:21.
6. Ephesians 2:10.
7. Gerhard Kittel, *Theological Dictionary of the New Testament*, vol. VI, (Grand Rapids, MI: Eerdmans Publishing Co., 1964), page 471.
8. Ephesians 5:2, emphasis added.
9. Ephesians 5:21, emphasis added.
10. Ephesians 5:22, emphasis added.
11. Ephesians 5:25, emphasis added.

12. Ephesians 6:1, emphasis added.
13. *Webster's New World Dictionary: Second College Edition*, ed. David B. Guralnic (Prentice-Hall, 1985), page 189.
14. *a.* Galatians 4:3; *b.* Gerhard Filledrich, *Theological Dictionary of the New Testament*, volume 7 (Grand Rapids, MI: Eerdmans, 1971), pages 679-687
15. Colossians 2:20-23.
16. Colossians 3:1-2.
17. John 3;19-21.
18. Zechariah 3:1-4.

CHAPTER 7

Change—How Hard It Is!

W hen the sinful nature makes its pitch to us it appeals to our sensuality—the desires of our five senses. It says, "Look at that! Wouldn't you like to have it! Take it. No one will know the difference. Smell that! Track it down. Taste it. Go ahead—eat the whole thing. What the heck—finish the bottle. Take her to bed; it will feel good!"

Temptation. Desirable and deadly. We waver on the brink of "No, I won't" and "Yes, I will." It's clear in our minds: We know that it's wrong and that it could ruin our lives. But then all of a sudden it's not that clear anymore. "I need this," the mind reasons. "No one's going to know. I'll do it just this once and get rid of this craving." We give in, and oh, how bitter it is. We have deceived ourselves again with our rationalizations that we knew all along were false.

We know that the more we say yes to our sensuality, the more it demands. We feed it, hoping it will go away, all the while knowing it will soon return all the stronger. Thus sensuality takes over. "All of us lived . . . at one time, gratifying the cravings of our sinful nature, and following its desires and thoughts."[1]

Jesus was right: "Everyone who sins is a slave to sin."[2] Sin eventually leaves even the most hardened unbeliever bored with life and disgusted with himself. Yet he continues like a robot, even while he knows that judgment stands at the end of his road.

Sin is a bad deal. It trades a moment of gratification for a lifetime—an eternity!—of alienation. Yet we buy it.

WHY DO WE STILL SIN WHEN WE KNOW IT'S THE WORST DEAL IN TOWN?

We do it for three reasons:

- It's our natural behavior.
- We program ourselves for it.
- We're blind to it.

It's Our Natural Behavior

Man didn't invent evil, but it didn't take him long to learn how to create it once he got started. Jesus said, "From within, out of men's hearts, come evil thoughts, sexual immorality, theft, murder, adultery, greed, malice, deceit, lewdness, envy, slander, arrogance and folly. All these evils come from inside and make a man 'unclean.' "[3]

According to this statement, if you and I found ourselves in an idyllic environment, unmarred by evil, it wouldn't take us long to put an end to its perfection. We could corrupt it even without the help of our circle of bad friends. We wouldn't even need the devil's help. It's all right there inside us.

Why do we sin? It's because we can't do otherwise. We just naturally pollute as we go along.

We Program Ourselves to Sin

Sigmund Freud's thesis is that there are three central parts in the mind: the id, the ego, and the superego.

The *id* consists of our primitive instincts and the residue of our memories. It is a wholly unconscious part of the mind. Yet it drives us.

The *ego* is partly conscious, partly unconscious. While the id is instinct-driven, the ego is driven by perceptions. It takes in the external world and decides what can and cannot pass through. So the ego determines our responses to a situation.

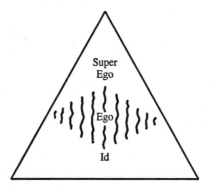

The *superego* exerts control over the ego by repressing it with the conscience—or unconscious guilt. Our heritage, from our parents, religion, teachers, and society, resides in the superego. It is the moral censor of the mind, the final editor of our behavior.[4]

It is hard to find much common ground between Jesus and Freud. But Freud happened on to some things Jesus had taught centuries earlier.

First, Freud observed in human behavior the same truth Jesus taught in Mark 4: that it is out of our hearts that evil thoughts, sexual immorality, etc., come. He just didn't call such things sin. He said they are expressions of our primitive instincts and unconscious memories.

He also happened on to something else Jesus had taught. Jesus said, "For out of the overflow of the heart the mouth speaks. The good man brings good things out of the good stored up in him, and the evil man brings evil things out of the evil stored up in him."[5]

Jesus is saying we program ourselves to sin. The things we do, the way we respond, our words, come out of the storehouse of our minds. In short, our behavior reflects the things our mind has been feeding on. That's the message of Freud's thesis as well. Only, when it comes to defining what is good and what is evil, Jesus and Freud are not even on the same map.

So, why do we sin? We program ourselves for it. James writes, "Each one is tempted when, by his own evil desire, he is dragged away and enticed. Then, after desire has conceived, it gives birth to sin; and sin, when it is full-grown, gives birth to death."[6] The image is of a pregnancy. Plant a seed of sinful desire, keep it around, nourishing it in your mind. In time you cannot *not* do that sin. It is true that the things we are entertaining in our minds today determine what we will be in the future.

We Are Blind and Irrational

This is one behavioral influence that Freud missed, along with all the other architects of enlightenment thought. In fact, this is the last thing they would ever bring themselves to admit! It is one of the most extraordinary truths about human nature that we find in the Bible. We are blind and irrational. We live contradictory, sinful lives because we cannot think clearly enough to do otherwise.

In Isaiah God said,

"Go and tell this people:
'Be ever hearing, but never understanding;
    be ever seeing, but never perceiving.'
Make the heart of this people calloused;
    make their ears dull
    and close their eyes.
Otherwise they might see with their eyes,
    hear with their ears,
    understand with their hearts,
and turn and be healed."[7]

Our first reaction to this statement is to protest against its apparent unfairness. Why on earth would God want a thing like that: to make people so dull that they can't understand enough to turn to Him? Doesn't He want everybody to come to Him?

But this was no slip of the pen. In fact, this prophecy is probably the most often repeated of all prophecies in all of Scripture. Jesus quoted it, and all four of the evangelists recorded it. Paul quoted it twice: in the last verses in the book of Acts and again in his letter to the Romans.

To get the full meaning of this prophecy, we need to lay these passages side by side and examine them together.[8] It quickly becomes obvious that this blindness and deafness is something we do to ourselves. The true cause is our rebellion. When we refuse to respond to the things God does reveal to us, we go deaf and blind to all the rest. Matthew says, "For this people's heart has become calloused; they hardly hear with their ears, and *they have closed their eyes.*"[9] The writer of the book of Hebrews repeatedly warns us that this could still happen to us! He says,

"Today, if you hear his voice,
　　do not harden your hearts
as you did in the rebellion,
　　during the time of testing in the desert."[10]

This blindness to sin transforms man into a highly irrational, very dangerous creature. We can live totally contradictory lives, and be oblivious to it all. We can kill and destroy, yet at the same time be convinced that we are the good guys and that right is on our side. Any history book or newspaper will quickly verify this fact.

In Isaiah 44, Isaiah creates a little scenario that dramatizes what we're talking about. The scenario begins with a man out in the forest. He is planting a tree. Then, for years he takes care of it and watches it grow. Finally, one day he takes his ax, goes into the forest, and chops the tree down. He drags it back to his workshop, where he trims off the branches and cuts them up for kindling. Then he takes his hammer and chisel to the trunk. He begins carving an image. Finally, satisfied with his work, he gathers the chips and branches and carries them to the kitchen. He carries the image into his living room and sets it on a shelf. He bows down to it and says, "Save me. You are my god."[11]

Then Isaiah editorializes:

> They know nothing, they understand nothing;
>> their eyes are plastered over so they cannot see,
>> and their minds closed so they cannot understand.
> No one stops to think,
>> no one has the knowledge or understanding to say,
> "Half of it I used for fuel;
>> I even baked bread over its coals,
>> I roasted meat and I ate.
> Shall I make a detestable thing from what is left?
>> Shall I bow down to a block of wood?"
> He feeds on ashes, a deluded heart misleads him;
>> he cannot save himself, or say,
>> "Is not this thing in my right hand a lie?"[12]

This irrationality surrounds us. It is present in the contradictions of the intellectuals that formulated our Western civilization. Not only do they contradict themselves with their ideas; their private lives are contradictions of their messages.

This irrationality is also present in the work of our scientists who wear a disguise of objectivity but defend their biases at all cost. Our legislators, economists, and educators all suffer from this same deception. And, of course, you and I are afflicted as well.

The human mind is the most amazing piece of work in all of God's creation, but by our rebelliousness we have diminished its usefulness. Sin has made the mind untrustworthy as a guide on anything of major significance.

So Why Do We Still Find Sin So Alluring?

We have just examined three powerful factors that ensure sin's future. It will be a part of our lives down to the end, and we will continue to fall into it! We'll go back to our diagram of Freud's concept of the mind to visualize what we've said.

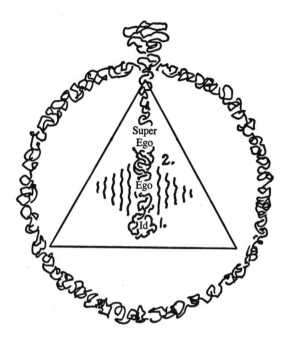

1. Sinful behavior is our natural behavior. It is there inside us. We have our own internal pollution mechanism that contaminates us, and the people around us.
2. We collect sin and store it in our hearts. We might forget that it's there, but when we open our mouths, that's what comes out.
3. We are blind and irrational. Thick clouds of self-deception fog up our minds so that we cannot think clearly enough to stay out of self-destructive behavior.

Well, you say, this is a pretty pessimistic picture. Isn't there any good news? It all seems so impenetrable!

HOW CAN WE NOT SIN WITH ALL THIS AGAINST US?

There is good news.

Jesus said, "If you hold to my teaching . . . then you will

know the truth, and the truth will set you free."[13] The people listening to Him, displaying the irrationality we just described, were puzzled. They responded that since they had never been slaves, they didn't really think they needed the emancipation Jesus was offering.

Jesus replied, "I tell you the truth, everyone who sins is a slave to sin . . . so if the son sets you free, you will be free indeed."[14]

So there is a solution and it is in the truth that Jesus makes available to us.

In chapter 5 we looked at the changes that take place at conversion. One change that we mentioned was the effect conversion has on our relationship to sin. We gave the subject one sentence. We made the observation, "We're paid up," and then went on to other things. We need to stop here and see what that means. We'll finish this chapter by looking at what Christ does to the control sin has over us when we come to Him. Then in the next chapter we'll go further to see how our deliverance works out in practice.

Our New Relationship to Sin

The central passage in the Bible on this subject is in Paul's letter to the Romans: chapters 6, 7, and 8.

Paul starts out in chapter 6 by describing our relationship to sin once we have received Christ's righteousness. He says, "We died to sin."[15]

Now what does that mean, that we are dead to sin? Dead people can't move. They can't respond to anything. Their problems with sensuality are over because none of their senses are working. Is that what it means to be dead to sin? It would be nice to be that immune, wouldn't it? But unfortunately we're not. And we know that's not what the text teaches either because later it goes on to encourage us not to give in to sin any longer. So what does it mean to be dead to sin?

Being dead to sin means that the claim sin had on us has been met. According to God's law, the penalty for sin is death. So we died! Romans 6:3-8 says that when Christ was on that cross dying, we died too. When He was buried, we were buried with Him. And when He arose from the dead, we were raised with Him. His resurrected life is our life, and death can't touch it. So, like we said before, we're paid up.

Now, you say, that's wonderful news, but if that's the end of the story, I'm still stuck in that cloud-shrouded triangle! I need some miracles here to get me out of the mess I'm in. You're right! The good news continues.

No Longer Slaves

Jesus described us all as slaves to sin. Paul picks up on this here. He says that in this dying to sin we are freed from it. Our freedom was purchased. What that means is that we now have an option. Until this point, sin controlled us. We *had* to obey it.[16] We don't have to do that any longer. We are now free to respond to God. So He exhorts us, "Do not let sin reign in your mortal body so that you obey its evil desires. . . . Rather offer yourselves to God, as those who have been brought from death to life."[17]

I once rescued a twelve-year-old boy from drowning in a lake. He had swum out after a ball, and had vanished. His dad, who couldn't swim, paced the shore as I towed the boy in. After he was okay, the three of us sat on the bank. We were strangers, but something profound had happened. All three of us felt awkward. There was nothing to say. So I went my way. As I walked off I thought of this boy who had gone from death to life. It reminded me of the phrase, "Offer yourselves to God, as those who have been brought from death to life."[18] How else, other than offering ourselves to Him, I thought, could we express our gratitude for His rescuing us? Words alone can't do it. Dying to sin opens this option. We can express our thanks by offering ourselves to Him "as instruments of righteousness."[19]

We will be exploring this emancipation in detail in the next chapter, but we need to add one new factor to our diagram to register what we've said here. The Holy Spirit needs to be in this diagram now because He is the One who makes all the difference.

When the Holy Spirit comes into our lives, the first thing we will want to do is heed His instructions.

> Those who live in accordance with the Spirit have their minds set on what the Spirit desires. The mind of sinful man is death, but the mind controlled by the Spirit is life and peace.[20]

When this happens, when we live in accordance with the Spirit, He begins to shut down the pollution mechanism and starts cleaning up the environment, from the inside out. Then He goes to work on our mental diet. He prompts us to change what we feed our minds. As our mental diet changes, the destructive memories begin to fade beneath the truth. We begin to heal. And the clouds of self-deception part. "The word of God is living and active . . . it penetrates . . . it judges the thoughts and attitudes of the heart. Nothing in all creation is hidden from God's sight."[21]

The potential for deliverance and transformation is immeasurable.

QUESTIONS FOR THOUGHT

1. Does this chapter give you any insights into your own attempts to overcome habits or change your behavior?

2. This chapter identifies several obstacles that confront us when we attempt to change. Which of them can you most relate to as obstacles you have experienced?

3. Why does Christ have to be involved if we are to change?

NOTES

1. Ephesians 2:3.
2. John 8:34.
3. Mark 7:21-23.
4. Sigmund Freud, *The Ego and the Id* (New York, London: W.W. Norton and Co., 1960), pages 11-36.
5. Matthew 12:34-35.
6. James 1:14-15.
7. Isaiah 6:9-10.
8. Matthew 13:13-15; Mark 4:12; Luke 8:10; John 12:40-41; Acts 28:26-28; Romans 11:8. See also Ezekiel 12:1-2; Mark 8:18; John 8:43-47; Hebrews 3:8,15; 4:7; Ephesians 4:17-19.
9. Matthew 13:15.
10. Hebrews 3:7-8.
11. Isaiah 44:17.
12. Isaiah 44:18-20.
13. John 8:31-36.
14. John 8:31-36.
15. Romans 6:2.
16. Romans 6:2.
17. Romans 6:13.
18. Romans 6:13.
19. Romans 6:13.
20. Romans 8:5-6.
21. Hebrews 4:12-13.

CHAPTER 8

Seven Elements
of Spiritual Transformation

C hange is a hot topic, especially personal change. Nobody's satisfied. None of us is content with himself the way he is. We all know we don't manage our time very well, or our money. We don't know enough about anything. We're too fat. We eat the wrong foods. We're neglecting our cholesterol count and can't maintain our exercise program. We're codependent and have low self-esteem. Our self-image is at bottom. We become frantic just thinking about all the things we must stop doing—and begin doing. We just must change.

There are as many approaches to changing one's life as there are areas that—we're convinced—need changing. Most people have given up on new year's resolutions and have gone on to more advanced efforts like meditation, group therapy, positive thinking, or they buy a book on the subject on their way to catch a plane. Some of it works for some people; most of it doesn't.

The kind of change we're interested in is of different dimensions. It has to do with going from spiritual death to

103

spiritual life; from being broken to becoming a whole person; from being destructive to being redemptive. It involves a change in one's very nature. Such changes are beyond the range of the self-help books and programs. We need *God's* help. We must be very clear on this.

This book is written to the insider, those followers of Christ who find their God-given sphere of service in the midst of the normal course of life. The arena in which we work is among our relationships. It is a unique arena, since every person has relationships with others that no one else has in quite the same way. Modern life has compounded the complexity of the insider's task. Our world is chaotic and we not only have to cope with holding everything together in our own lives; we need to have enough left over to give to the people around us. It is not an easy calling.

The purpose of this book is to help us as insiders understand the nature of our ministry, what it is we are called to do and how to go about it. We have identified our primary purpose as helping people know Christ and grow to maturity—to where they look and act like Christ. Thus, helping people to grow—to change—is at the heart of the insider's calling. That's why we are devoting so much attention to this subject here.

So far we have seen that this process of spiritual change begins with a supernatural transaction. Some things change immediately, permanently, at the time of that transaction. At the point of conversion the Holy Spirit moves into one's life as the primary change agent for the remainder of the journey.

We also saw how the kind of change we're dealing with is not merely behavior modification. It is not just stopping one set of practices to take on another. It focuses on the transformation of who we are in Christ and works its way on out, changing values—and then behavior.

Yet change is not easy. Christ has freed us from sin; we don't have to do it anymore. But nonetheless, we're in for a war as we attempt to leave our sinful behavior behind and change into the image of Christ.

This chapter, "Seven Elements of Spiritual Transformation,"

will hopefully help us as insiders to win our own personal war and also equip us to bring deliverance to the people God is giving us in our arena.

THE SEVEN ELEMENTS
OF SPIRITUAL TRANSFORMATION

The seven elements of spiritual transformation are:

- Experience
- The Scriptures
- Struggle
- Humility
- The Holy Spirit
- Self-control
- Community

I developed this subject briefly in *Church Without Walls*, but the intent of this book being what it is, I will be giving it a more thorough treatment here, including some revision.[1] We will explore each of these seven elements and see how they interact.

Experience

Experience is the matrix in which change is forged. Usually the realization that we have a need to change begins with an experience. Then when we take on the challenge of changing a particular behavior pattern, we must work it out in the arena of experience.

We all have experiences all the time. Some are good, some are bad, some are routine and incidental, some are decisive. Earlier we observed that the people of modernity come in a broken state. We ourselves are damaged and are having to deal with the effects, and likewise we will find an array of needs in the people in our arena that will demand attention. The experiences we are especially interested in here are those that are symptoms of deeper needs: things that reveal wrong attitudes, fears, destructive behaviors, and so on.

I was twenty years old when I got married. At that time I would have flunked the test on self-awareness. I was oblivious, with no idea that I traveled through life like a tank, going over or through whatever was in my path to get to where I was going. For me, there in my tank, everything was fine. But it was a hard ride for my bride. Often she came out with my tread marks all over her person.

I was very slow to catch on, partly because Marge is so gentle and patient. I spent the next several years charging ahead in my tank, oblivious to the fact that I was leaving her less and less space to be herself. Then I had an experience. Marge blew up! Some people blow up regularly, so the explosions have little effect anymore. It's, "There she blows again!" But this was different. It was a 10-point explosion that immediately had my full attention. We were in our car, and I can still, after all these years, take you back to the spot in the road where it happened.

I listened as Marge unloaded. She was right, I knew it, and I was devastated. That explosion has proven to be one of the most valuable experiences of my entire life. It was the beginning of a transformation process that continues to this day.

Can change ever happen apart from experience? We're never really sure. It takes experiences to road-test the progress we think we've made. To illustrate: The Apostle Paul found himself in a situation he was sure he would never survive to tell about. He wrote, "We were under great pressure, far beyond our ability to endure. Indeed, in our hearts we felt the sentence of death."

Paul tells us what he learned in the midst of that circumstance. "But this happened that we might not rely on ourselves but on God, who raises the dead."[2] Paul learned from this experience that there is no such thing as a hopeless situation with God.

As you and I read these words, we believe Paul and agree with his conclusion. But have we been changed, really? Probably not. We have been helped. His experience gives us something to hold on to when we find ourselves in our own "beyond hope" situation. It can encourage us to go to the same God for the same kind of rescue. Then when we've been through it, we'll know whether or not we have truly changed.

Any learning that takes place independent of experience does not go beyond academics. That is the kind of learning we get in school. Academic learning is important, but it can never be an end in itself. It is always only a starting point. An engineering student can do his course work. On graduation day he can call himself an engineer. But it will take *experience* to transform him into a competent professional.

Experiences do not guarantee change. Whether or not they contribute to our changing is up to us. It depends on our response. Hebrews 12:11 makes the point. "No discipline seems pleasant at the time, but painful. Later on, however, it produces a harvest of righteousness and peace *for those who have been trained by it.*"

So, experience is at the center of the change process. We now need to go on and explore what kind of response is necessary for change.

Our illustration of the change process begins with experience at the center.

The Scriptures

The appropriate response to an insight gained through experience is to turn to the Scriptures. When we're sorting through something that's happening, whether it's something good, a problem, a trial, or a decision we face, we have a special need for God's Word. Without it, we're unable to make sense of our experiences. The psalmist said, "Your word is a lamp to my feet and a light for my path."[3] Using the same metaphor, Jesus adds, "Everyone who does evil hates the light, and will not come to the light for fear that his deeds will be exposed. But whoever lives by the truth comes into the light, so that it may be seen plainly that what he has done has been done through God."[4]

The key word here is *truth*. God's Word is truth. To come to the Scriptures with our needs is to hold them up to the light of truth. God's Word illuminates. It penetrates our clouds of self-deception and shows things as they really are. It takes courage to step into the light in this way. To be confronted with the truth about ourselves can be like getting caught with no clothes on. But we must see things as they are before we can do what needs to be done.

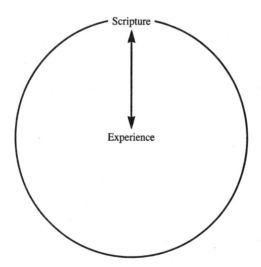

At times like these, the message from the Scriptures can be reinforced in any number of forms. It can be something from your memory. It might come from another believer who deliberately speaks to the issue. Sometimes it's a sermon where you go away thinking, "Someone must have told him about me!" The small group, where you open up about what's going on in your life, is another source. Sources such as these can get you started, can point you in the right direction in the Scriptures. But we need to go deeper, on our own.

How do we go about that? It takes more than just leafing through the Bible to find an appropriate verse or two. The approach that has helped me the most over the years has been to set aside time every day to read the Bible consecutively: something in the Old Testament, something in the New. A reading chart, which I keep in my Bible, helps me keep track of where I am. I pray as I read, asking God to give me understanding. When in the most unexpected places I come across something that addresses my situation, I stop to reflect. Clarity begins to replace my confusion. In the quiet I have heard God's instructions under the direction of the Holy Spirit. The learning experience may take a week; it may take six months or longer.

The process doesn't end there. It is possible to hear God's voice and do nothing about it. I still fail regularly at that point. James writes, "The man who looks intently into the perfect law that gives freedom, and continues to do this, not forgetting what he had heard, but doing it—he will be blessed in what he does."[5] When God gives us understanding, we need to be very careful to respond.

Struggle
Struggle is the next element in the process of spiritual transformation—*great* struggle. My behavior has just been confronted by truth—and war breaks out. I now know what is right. I know what I need to do, but am I going to do it? I want to do what's right, and I don't want to do what's right. My emotions, intellect, and will are back on the scene and are at each other's throats again. My emotions are protesting, "I don't feel like it." My intellect has

come up with reasons why, if I do it, the rest of my life will be damaged. And my will is busy making the final choice, knowing he always gets his way anyway. This infuriates the intellect, and drives the emotions into a frenzy.

Observe Paul's description of his inner wars in Romans 7. He tells how he encountered the truth in the law and set out to do it, but all his attempts ended in failure. He laments, "I do not understand what I do. For what I want to do I do not do, but what I hate I do. . . . I have the desire to do what is good, but I cannot carry it out. For what I do is not the good I want to do; no, the evil I do not want to do—this I keep on doing." He ends the passage with a cry to be rescued.[6]

We have already talked about this struggle in previous chapters. In chapter 5 we saw how civil war breaks out when the sinful nature is confronted by the new nature that has been given to us by the Holy Spirit. These two natures are natural enemies and will be in conflict right down to the end. "For the sinful nature desires what is contrary to the Spirit, and the Spirit what is contrary to the sinful nature. They are in conflict with each other, so that you do not do what you want."[7]

Our sensuality is the major battle supply line for our sinful nature. Most of my struggles with sin would be nonexistent if I had no sensual desires. But I have them, so the battle goes on.

Have you ever noticed how the Scriptures point out that false teachings or false doctrines aren't the result of someone's honest mistake in interpreting the Scriptures? Rather, they are elaborate creations for the sake of satisfying someone's sinful desires.[8] Sensuality is the driving force behind idolatry.[9]

We can probably all identify with the struggle I'm describing here. We know what we should do. We know the consequences of our choices. The question is, Which option will I choose? What side is going to win this battle? It can go one of three ways:

1. I can say no to the truth and persist in doing wrong.
2. I can say yes to the truth—and turn left.
3. I can say yes to the truth—and turn right.

We will have to go further into the chapter before we can make sense of that left-turn option. It's a wrong turn. What we're interested in here is understanding what it means to turn right.

The person who turns right, sees his need for change, understands what the Scriptures have to say on the matter, and responds properly. James writes, "The man who looks intently into the perfect law that gives freedom, and continues to do this, not forgetting what he has heard, but doing it—he will be blessed in what he does."[10] A proper response is to be attentive to God's Word, retaining it and acting accordingly. This response requires a certain attitude on our part. It is *humility*. In the same passage James says, "Humbly accept the word planted in you, which can save you."[11] This brings us to our fourth element of spiritual transformation.

Humility

"Heaven is my throne,
    and the earth is my footstool.
Where is the house you will build for me?
    Where will my resting place be?
Has not my hand made all these things,
    and so they came into being?" declares the LORD.
"This is the one I esteem:
    he who is humble and contrite in spirit,
    and trembles at my word."[12]

Isaiah summarizes what we have said so far in this section. Does it surprise you that humility is the response God is watching for? How about repentance, or confession? Humility precedes them both. Neither can happen without humility.

Humility is the one response I am still capable of making even when I am at my worst, even while I'm in the midst of struggle. It is an admission of my weakness and dependence. The Holy Spirit responds to this admission. He comes in and empowers me to respond to the current struggle in His favor.

There can be no deliverance without humility. It takes humility to be honest and come clean. How difficult it is to say, "I was wrong!" But these words take us out of our darkness and into the light. They bring us out into the open before God and our sisters and brothers. Humility sets the stage for the Holy Spirit's direction and empowerment. Once our old natures have been subdued, reason and truth can have a voice. As we humble ourselves, God can quit resisting us and begin to hear us instead.[13]

There is an unbelievable illustration of the power of humility in 2 Chronicles 33. Manasseh was the most perverse king in Judah's history. He built altars to the Baals and made Asherah poles. He worshiped the stars, building altars to them in the Temple itself! He made human sacrifices of his own sons, and practiced sorcery, divination, and witchcraft. He consulted mediums and spiritists. He even put a carved image in the Holy Place of the Temple. The passage says Manasseh led the people astray "so that they did more evil than the nations the LORD had destroyed before the Israelites."[14]

So what did God do? He warned Manasseh. But Manasseh didn't listen, so God took another step. He sent the Assyrian army. They made Manasseh a prisoner, ran a hook through his nose, bound him in shackles, and marched him off to Babylon. Manasseh was in pain. Now to quote the passage: "In his distress he sought the favor of the LORD his God and *humbled* himself greatly before the God of his fathers. And when he prayed to him, the LORD was moved . . . so he brought him back to Jerusalem and to his kingdom."[15]

Apparently there is no mess that can become so bad that it can't be resolved when we genuinely humble ourselves. When we humble ourselves, God can move in and help us. Until we do, we're on our own.

Prayer and worship are the language of humility. It's the language God responds to. The angel told Daniel, "Since the first day that you set your mind to gain understanding *and to humble yourself before God*, your words were heard, and I have come in response to them."[16] Worship is also a part of our response, for to worship God is to offer our being to Him in acknowledgment of who He is. Pride and worship cannot exist together. Worship cleanses and prepares us for what comes next.

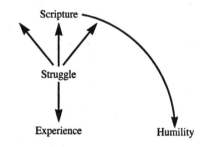

The Holy Spirit

The Holy Spirit is the fifth element in our process of spiritual transformation. He responds when we humble ourselves by empowering us to be and do what we could never achieve without Him. I have found Philippians 2:13 to be one of the most useful verses in the Bible: "For it is God who works in you to *will* and to *act* according to his good purpose." Frequently I find my will and my actions are running contrary to God's purposes. I also find that, at those times, I don't have it in me to turn my wrong set of attitudes off and switch over to wanting to do God's purposes. What I can do is ask God to empower me to make those changes according to this promise. Then I wait. The attitude changes. It doesn't work quite as fast as our TV channel changer, but it does happen.

Not long ago I had a conversation with a young Muslim. We were talking about knowing God, and it was apparent that this was something he greatly desired. For the Muslim, Allah is distant and impersonal. At one point in the conversation he asked, "What can I do to control the enticements of my flesh?" He was experiencing the struggles we talked about earlier, and was on the losing end.

Everything I have described to this point about spiritual transformation is possible, to a degree, for this young Muslim. He can seek to understand his experiences in light of the Bible. It would be conceivable for him to humble himself and admit his wrongdoing. If he would do those things, he would benefit. Life would be better for him. But he would never, with that, experience deliverance. I told him so.

The Holy Spirit is the One who makes the way of Christ distinct from every other way. The libraries are full of philosophies that, if followed, would greatly improve a person's life. They would bring order and structure. The religions of the world all make utopian promises. But they cannot deliver. The Holy Spirit delivers. He keeps all His promises. He doesn't just give us good advice on how we ought to live; He empowers us to live that life out.

So we add the Holy Spirit to our diagram.

Self-Control

The sixth element of spiritual transformation is self-control. I have vacillated over which word to use to identify this element. We could use the word *obedience*. It is a broad, familiar word in our

Christian vocabulary. But *self-control* is more precise and carries with it the smell of the battle we have been describing.

Peter exhorts his readers to "prepare your minds for action; be self-controlled."[17] In his second letter he begins with a list of qualities that should emerge as we grow in faith. Self-control is in the middle of that list. Titus identifies self-control as being one of the essential qualities for an elder. The word used in these passages is *egkrate*. It means strength, having power over, holding oneself in.

This self-control is not *self*-control. It's not the kind you read about in the paperbacks. This self-control comes from the Holy Spirit, as the characteristics of the fruit of the Spirit in Galatians 5:22-23 shows.

We are not condemned to spend our lives in a losing struggle against our old patterns of behavior. As we understand ourselves through the Scriptures, and as we win in our struggles against sin by humbly confessing our weakness, the Holy Spirit empowers us to respond in new ways. He ministers to us in two areas: in the "I will" and in the "I can." The "I will" is the choice I make to obey God; the "I can" is the ability to follow through on that choice with my actions. So, the next time the old, well-worn patterns of behavior come around, we can declare our emancipation from them and take an alternative route into freedom.

This to me is a most fascinating paradox. We are strong, not because we are strong but because we are weak. We can control our behavior only because we have learned we cannot. Paul enjoyed living in this paradox. He said, "I delight in weaknesses, in insults, in hardships, in persecutions, in difficulties. For when I am weak, then I am strong." He was strong because his admissions to his weakness opened the way for the power of Christ to rest on him.[18]

This empowering toward self-control by the Holy Spirit opens a new option for us. Formerly we lived lives that were so out of control we couldn't do what was right even when our lives depended on it. We can't blame others for that, nor can we call it fate. We *willed* our way into this bondage. Now we are free to choose, to choose an alternate response.

- Where the usual response was anger, this time it can be patience. And when we lose it, the humility can be there to ask for forgiveness.
- Where lust has been the habit, respect for the person can take its place. In case of relapse, transparency can restore.
- Where impatience has always ruled the day, understanding can take its place.
- Anxiety can be replaced by confidence. When it's not there, the healthy attitude is to admit it.

As we choose the godly response, we will find that the Holy Spirit comes to our aid and empowers us to fulfill it.

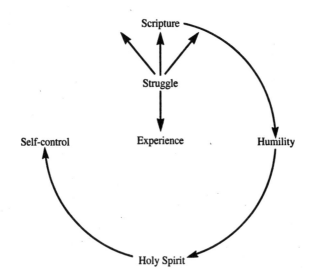

A single victory does not put an end to the war. There will be pain and ambivalence as we give up our old habits. They were desire-driven, and some of those desires will die hard. But freedom becomes more satisfying with every victorious choice. So, we make a circle. It takes repeated victories to replace old habits with new ones.

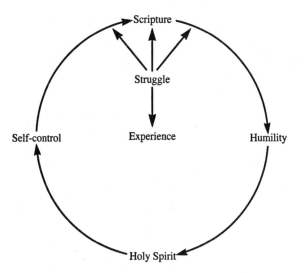

So, what about that left turn?

The Left-Turn Option

Earlier in the chapter we noted that we end the "Yes, I will"/"No, I won't" struggle by making one of three decisions.

I can end it by saying no to the truth and continue to go on unchanged. Or, I can say yes to the truth, and turn right. This is a very humiliating route because the first stop is to admit how weak you are and ask for help. Our old nature hates this! Then the Holy Spirit moves in and enables us. What this route has going for it is that it is the right road. It's the only way to get there from where you are.

There is a third option that does have certain advantages. It allows you to stay on the side of truth and also preserve your independence. It involves going to the Bible, understanding what it says about your experience and what needs to be done. Then you just set out and do it. You turn left under your own power. There are no humiliating admissions involved, and your pride stays intact. It's quite nice.

But—you have just taken a wrong turn. The right turn is the "grace route." The left turn is the "do it in the flesh route." No one ever got there by turning left. "Are you so foolish? After beginning with the Spirit, are you now trying to attain your goal by human effort?"[19] When you turn left, you end up in failure.

The seventh element of spiritual transformation is also critical. We can do all the rest, but if this seventh element isn't there, progress will be minimal.

Community

The Epistles are filled with statements that remind us of our interdependence with one another as God's people. We are told to be devoted to one another, to live in harmony with one another, to love one another, to stop passing judgment, and to bear with each other's failings. We are to accept and to serve one another.[20] Statements such as these go on and on, literally scores of them throughout the New Testament. Their prominence underscores the extent of our need for our brothers and sisters in Christ.

A Christian must have an environment where he or she can go and talk openly about how things are going in this matter of following Christ. It needs to be a place where one can get personalized attention, and give it to others.

The transformation process we have been describing is characterized by struggle. Nobody can stick it out in an effort of this nature, day after day, year after year, if they attempt to go it alone. Hebrews 3:13 says, "Encourage one another daily, as long as it is called today, so that none of you may be hardened by sin's deceitfulness."

This passage implies an intense, daily, accepting environment, where the experiences we are dealing with can be an open topic of conversation. It implies commitment to one another, being there when the going gets heavy, when a sister or brother is more inclined to choose wrong over right. All of us find ourselves in that mode at times. Some of us are on the edge of it most of the time. More than anything else, we need the cheering section on these occasions. We also need the prayers of others.

James instructs us, "Confess your sins to each other and pray for each other so that you may be healed."[21] Honesty, mutual loving support, and intercession for one another are essential ingredients to repairing the damage in our lives.

A community such as we have just described is small, port-able, and fluid. It is of such a nature that we, as insiders, can take it with us, or operate out of it. We will be discussing this subject more thoroughly in chapter 11.

So we complete our illustration of the elements of spiritual transformation by including *community.*

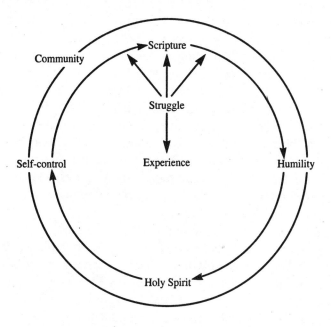

GUIDELINES FOR HELPING OTHERS IN THIS PROCESS

This process we have just described needs to be very clear in your mind. Test it against your own experiences in growth and change. In that way, the seven elements begin to function as a frame of reference. The following suggestions are intended to help you as you serve others.

- Help the new believer understand the things he or she is experiencing. Ask questions and listen carefully to the answers. Be genuinely interested. Be *very* slow to give advice at this stage. Refrain from sharing your favorite chapter and verse on the subject. The most important thing at this point is to get the experience out into the light so that it can be understood for what it is.

■ Teach the person how to listen to God on the matter. Suggest a passage, or a book of the Bible. Get this person started in reading, meditating, and praying over the Scriptures. Help him or her organize the time for this if that is a problem. Make sure the person sticks to the Bible rather than going to "a good book on the subject." The person needs to learn to listen to God's voice.

■ Encourage the person to journal his or her thoughts. He or she needs to record what he or she is experiencing and learning. Specific needs should be written down as matters for prayer. This helps bring objectivity into the process. A journal should not become something burdensome. It doesn't require daily entries, and notes can be very brief. In time this journal becomes one's personal "book of the Acts."

■ Use your knowledge of the person's situations for prayer. Pray specifically, according to Philippians 4:6-7 and encourage him or her to do the same. Pray together. Be careful not to be manipulative with your prayers (for example, "I'm praying God will give you wisdom to get out of this relationship"). Keep informed on progress toward answers.

■ Do not judge. Accept the person as he or she is, problems and all. Take failures in stride. Remember, failures are not the problem. It is the attitudes that produce the failures that need transforming. This work should be left to the Holy Spirit.

■ Be transparent yourself. Let your weaknesses show. Any true relationship is a two-way street. Let the person see the process at work in your own life.

■ Make sure the person has access to community as we described it in this chapter. It may be necessary to initiate something for him or her. It could be three or four couples in a neighborhood, a half-dozen singles, or a mix of singles and couples.

NOTES

 1. Jim Petersen, *Church Without Walls* (Colorado Springs, CO: NavPress, 1992), pages 195-203.
 2. 2 Corinthians 1:8-9.
 3. Psalm 119:105.
 4. John 3:20-21.
 5. James 1:25.
 6. Romans 7:9-25.
 7. Galatians 5:17.
 8. Romans 16:18, Philippians 3:19, 2 Timothy 4:3
 9. 1 Corinthians 10:6-9.
10. James 1:25.
11. James 1:21.
12. Isaiah 66:1-2.
13. 1 Peter 5:5.
14. 2 Chronicles 33:9.
15. 2 Chronicles 33:12-13.
16. Daniel 10:12.
17. 2 Peter 1:5.
18. 2 Corinthians 12:9-10.
18. Galatians 3:3.
20. Romans 12:10-16; 13:8; 15:1.
21. James 5:16.

CHAPTER 9

When Bad Things Happen: Understanding Suffering and Adversity

When Bad Things Happen to Good People. If you are any kind of a bookstore browser you have probably seen this title by Rabbi Harold Kushner on the stands. It catches your attention, probably because you've had the same question. You move on and the question is there for a moment in your mind: Why *do* bad things happen to good people?

Insiders often need to deal with this question. It is going to come up. It has already come up in our own lives again and again. And as we become increasingly involved in other people's lives, we will see that suffering and adversity are a part of virtually every life. The question is kept alive by the ample nourishment it receives from the things we experience and watch other people go through.

We all know people who have suffered real tragedy sometime in their lives. Perhaps it was a teenage son who was killed by a drunken driver. Or it might have been a husband who died of cancer, leaving a wife on her own with three small children.

123

It could have been an accident that left someone permanently disabled.

Some people experience tragedies of this nature and work through them in a positive way, coming out of them stronger than ever. There is something about them—they are the kind of people you turn to when a crisis of your own comes around.

Others who suffer tragedies are still angry years later. They take their anger to bed with them at night, stay awake with it, and get up with it in the morning. They have nurtured their anger to where it is now bitterness. It drives their lives. They are still mad at the drunken driver. They are mad at the police department and at the judiciary system. But they are especially mad at God. Always, just below the surface, lies the question, "Why did God allow it to happen?"

This is a fair question, and an ancient one. If God is all-powerful, and if He's good, why all this evil? And why do the *innocent* suffer from it? The psalmists and the prophets asked this question. Philosophers and theologians have struggled with it. Poets and writers have taken their inspiration from it.

I have friends who refuse to believe in Christ because they cannot find a satisfactory answer to this question. I know Christians who have stalled out in their spiritual progress because they feel overwhelmed by the proliferation of evil around them and can't figure out why God doesn't do more than He is doing to keep it in check. I myself walk the razor's edge between faith and confusion as my work takes me into the parts of the world where there is nothing but agony and darkness. I watch my children, now in their twenties, working toward a realistic understanding of what they should and should not expect of God.

GETTING A RIGHT PICTURE OF GOD

The real issue behind these questions we struggle with is that God is not measuring up to our expectations. That makes us wonder about His justice. That, of course, is the question behind the question: *Is God just?* He certainly does not seem to be living up to the things we learned about Him. We learned that:

- God is perfect; He is holy.
- He is just.
- He is the creator of all that exists.
- He is the sovereign ruler over all.
- He has infinite wisdom and power.
- A sparrow can't fall without His knowledge. He knows how many hairs we have on our heads.
- He loves us.

I believe all these statements to be true. The problem comes as we attempt to add them together. The sum of them doesn't correspond to reality. If all of these things are true, we ask, How is it that hatred and greed apparently have full run of the entire world? How is it that violence and injustice seem to be in control? This disparity between our theology and reality is a recipe for disillusionment.

We attempt to cope with this disparity in various ways. Some of us just spiritualize everything. It's mysterious, we agree, but somehow everything that is happening is the will of God. Others among us sort of withdraw. This shows up in our prayer lives. We refrain from going after anything of significance in prayer because God doesn't seem to be doing a very good job in responding. We're afraid to ask because we're afraid He won't answer. And if He doesn't answer, that will raise one more question we'll have to add to the list. We're afraid to put our faith to work because we fear God will fail the test. As followers of Christ, we go on the inactive list.

GETTING THE REST OF THE STORY

It is not God that is at the root of these problems; it is our theology. Most simply put, theology is the study of God. We should all be theologians!

Our little description of God is incomplete. It is, in fact, just a fragment of the whole picture. All of us have a notion of God and what He's like. It's made up of bits and pieces we've picked up here and there. We have composed these pieces, like a mosaic, into a picture of Him that we carry around with us. One thing we can be sure of. Our pictures are inaccurate. Some of the pieces we use don't even belong. As Paul said, "Now we see but a poor reflection; then we shall see face to face. Now I know in part; then I shall know fully."[1]

As we go through a difficult experience, we take out our snapshots of God and look at them. We want to reassure ourselves that with Him being who He is, everything is going to be okay. What we see, however, is not always all that reassuring. It doesn't occur to us that the problem might be with the snapshot, that it's just a caricature of who God really is. Since God is not going to perform according to how we imagine Him to be but according to His true self, we find Him unpredictable. We end up having doubts about Him and His reliability. This is one more reason why increasing in our knowledge of God should be the primary pursuit of our lives.[2]

So let's go on to the rest of the story. Before we can make progress toward understanding the problem of evil and suffering, we need to add a few more basic observations to our list. We just need to remember, when we've done our best to put it all together here, we're still peering at a poor reflection of the real thing! We will still be missing some pieces.

- God created the earth, and then gave it to man. Man was given rulership over the natural world. "God said, 'Let us make man in our image, in our likeness, and let them rule over . . . all the earth, and over all the creatures that move along the ground.'" He gave His creation to man to use and to control. (Genesis 1:26-30; see Psalm 8). Man has the responsibility to maintain order and make proper use of the natural world.
- God gave man the freedom and the capacity to make his own choices. "The LORD God commanded the man, 'You are free to . . . but you must not.'" Then the passage goes on: "Now the LORD God had formed . . . all the beasts of the field and all the birds of the air. He brought them to the man to see what he would name

them; and whatever the man called each living creature, that was its name" (Genesis 2:16-20). From the very beginning, man could choose how he would relate to God, and he was given decision-making power over the natural world. Man has a God-given dominion, a space of his own where his decisions stand.

■ The natural world as we know it is not the same as it was before the fall of humankind. "The creation waits in eager expectation for the sons of God to be revealed. For the creation was subjected to frustration, not by its own choice, but by the will of the one who subjected it, in the hope that the creation itself will be liberated from its bondage to decay. . . . We know that the whole creation has been groaning as in the pains of child-birth right up to the present time" (Romans 8:19-22). Nature itself is in decay as a result of sin entering the world.

■ Satan has a usurped dominion, a rulership. At the temptation in the wilderness, he offered Jesus the authority and splendor of all the kingdoms of the world, explaining, "for it has been given to me, and I can give it to anyone I want to" (Luke 4:6). This was a claim Jesus didn't dispute! Jesus Himself called Satan "The prince of this world" (John 12:31). The Apostle John stated that "The whole world is under the control of the evil one" (1 John 5:19).

■ Satan rules over the ungodly. Paul writes, "You followed the ways of this world and of the ruler of the kingdom of the air, the spirit who is now at work in those who are disobedient" (Ephesians 2:2). Salvation, says Paul, is being "rescued from the *dominion of darkness* and brought . . . into the kingdom of the Son" (Colossians 1:13).

We still have not considered all of the factors necessary for us to understand what is going on in the world. But let's pause here and consider some of the implications of these additional truths we've just seen. The problem of evil, suffering, and adversity has begun to make sense.

God created the earth. He made man with the freedom to choose. He made him the ruler of the natural world. Man's decision to rebel, his fall, affected the natural world, causing it to begin to decay.[3] Satan gained control of what was originally man's dominion, and he now rules. If these things are true, what kind of a world should we expect? We should expect just about what we're getting!

So we have some answers. But we have also raised some new questions. For me, I'm confronted now with two new questions. One has to do with God's sovereignty; the other has to do with the nature of Satan's rulership. We'll take the one on Satan first.

As to Satan's rule, are we saying that Satan and God are at war, that there are two kingdoms in conflict, the kingdom of God and the kingdom of Satan? Is this not beginning to sound like a form of dualism: a good God and an evil devil fighting it out?

That is not at all what the Bible teaches. The outcome of Satan's rebellion against God has never been in question. The sphere of his rule has always been contained within specific limits. Satan does not have a kingdom at all; he has a dominion. He is nobody's king, but he dominates people and their political/economic systems.

Christ's death and resurrection was Satan's death knell. His days are numbered. Just before He went to the cross, Jesus said, "Now is the time for judgment on this world; now the prince of this world will be driven out."[4] I wonder if the scenario in Revelation 12:7-12 does not describe the impact of Christ's death on Satan's position. This passage describes Satan losing his place in heaven—"that ancient serpent called the devil, or Satan, who leads the whole world astray. He was hurled to the earth, and his angels with him." Then someone announces:

"Now have come the salvation and the power and the
         kingdom of our God,
      and the authority of his Christ.
For the accuser of our brothers,

who accuses them before our God day and night,
has been hurled down. . . .
Therefore rejoice, you heavens
and you who dwell in them!
But woe to the earth and the sea,
because the devil has gone down to you!
He is filled with fury,
because he knows that his time is short."[5]

Throughout the Old Testament we find Satan having access to God's presence. According to this passage he loses that somewhere along the line. Was Jesus not saying on His way to the cross that that was precisely what was about to happen? Did He not say, "Now the prince of this world will be driven out"?[6] I think that war took place on the day Christ rose from the dead and ascended back into Heaven. When Satan was driven out he focused his fury on our world. It was a time of celebration in heaven, but a time of mourning for us.

If this is what this passage means, it explains a lot. The evil of our day is of such incredible proportions it has got to be inspired.

Now, what about the other question concerning God's sovereignty? Where is God while all this evil is going on? Is He merely a passive observer? By no means! But He *is* honoring His commitment to man. Within creation, man has a dominion, a rulership, a freedom. God hasn't gone back on that, although through man's sinfulness he has forfeited virtually all His authority to Satan.

Apparently there is a threshold of injustice that God will not allow a nation to cross. When a certain point of perversion and corruption is reached, God says, "That's it! Time's up!" and judgment becomes inevitable. We see this occurring repeatedly in the Old Testament, and we see it verified as secular history unfolds. Where did all the great empires of the past go? How and why did they collapse? God retains the ultimate word where Satan, man, and society are concerned. He restricts Satan,[7] keeps the unrighteous in check,[8] judges the nations,[9] and controls history.[10] We may think He should be exercising a lot more control than He does as we watch the world tearing itself apart, but that's our view as seen through the "poor reflection."

We ask, Why doesn't God put an end to all this evil? God replies, Just wait and see.

Evil was around before the world began but it won't be after it is gone. Even before the creation of the universe, God had His work all planned out. The centerpiece of His creation was to be a people: the church. He knew, because of evil, it would require a Cross to beget that people. Yet He created (Ephesians 1:3-10).

God has displayed His generosity in His creation. He created the world, and gave it to man. When man fell, He promised salvation. He gave us the prophets, who gave us God's Word. He gave His Son, who gave His life. He gave us membership in His family. He gave us the Holy Spirit. And one day He will give us His Kingdom![11] God is a giver.

As for evil, it is in its death throes. Why doesn't God do something about all this evil? we repeat. The answer is, He has done it, and He is doing it. The day is coming when "He [Christ] hands over the kingdom to God the Father after he has destroyed all dominion, authority and power."[12]

THE ORIGINS OF SUFFERING AND ADVERSITY

All of what we have said so far in this chapter is necessary as background to our question: Why do bad things happen to good people? As we reflect on the things we've said, it becomes apparent that suffering and adversity come into our lives from many sources other than God. We will look at several of them here.

Sin Brings Suffering

Sin is the most obvious, certain source of pain and adversity. The first sin resulted in the expulsion of Adam and Eve from Paradise, and life has never been utopian anywhere again from that day to this. Sin brings death. It brings not just spiritual death, but death of every sort. Relationships die, our aspirations and expectations die. And our bodies die. Our sinful choices produce dark effects.

Sometimes we find ourselves on the receiving end of other

people's sinful actions. The excess of the drunken driver that killed the sixteen-year-old son was sin. Sinful acts will bring suffering to the Christian and nonChristian alike.

Bad Judgment Can Cause Suffering

When we make bad decisions we have to live with the consequences. "He who scorns instruction will pay for it, but he who respects a command is rewarded."[13]

When a Christian makes a bad decision, he will suffer the consequences just like anyone else. A hasty decision on a marriage partner will leave a person with plenty of time to regret it. God is not obligated to make a poorly conceived business deal work for you just because you're a Christian.

While I was in college I invested in some property through a real estate firm without first gathering adequate information on the business practices of the company. Later, when the owners of the company were taken to court for misuse of federal funds, I found myself in financial trouble. My money was tied up for several months and I struggled to pay my bills.

It would hardly have been appropriate for me to complain to God that He wasn't doing a very good job of supplying my needs. The problem was, I wasn't doing a good job of running my financial affairs!

Just Living in the Natural World and Being Subject to Its Laws Can Bring Suffering and Adversity

If you walk across the street and get hit by a car, your being a Christian will have no influence on the extent of your injuries. The laws of physics have the same effect on everyone. We don't get a perfect immune system at conversion. The Christian is as subject to disease and aging as anyone else. If I am on a trip and am bitten by a malaria-carrying mosquito and later get the fever, nausea, and chills that come with the disease, the question would not be, "Why did God allow this to happen?" It would be more appropriate to ask, "Why didn't I use the mosquito netting that was hanging there, right over the bed?"

Many bad things happen just because we are subject to the

laws of a material world, of which sickness and disease are a part.

Just Being a Part of Society Can Cause Us Suffering and Adversity

The sins of a few people often cause great suffering on a national scale. For instance, many societies today struggle with uncontrolled inflation. It is not uncommon for inflation to reach forty percent per month. Virtually without exception, the cause is corruption among public officials who are in league with industries in the private sector. Their greed is of such proportions that they are unfazed by the fact that they are impoverishing millions of their fellow citizens.

I know people whose businesses were ruined in 1986 by the changes in the US tax laws. They are still trying to pick up the pieces. In this case the suffering was caused not by group sin but by a group's misjudgment.

Faith in Christ doesn't exempt us from the consequences of the political and economic turns taken by the society we live in.

Suffering and Adversity Can Be Inflicted by Satan Himself

"The devil . . . prompted Judas Iscariot, son of Simon, to betray Jesus."[14] Later on in the evening, Jesus gave Judas a piece of bread. "As soon as Judas took the bread, Satan entered into him."[15] Satan orchestrated the events that took Jesus to the cross.

Since Satan rules over the ungodly, it should come as no surprise that we will suffer at his hands through his people.

Not long ago I participated in a Bible study in an African city. It was on a Tuesday night, so we wanted to keep it short. Everyone had to be up early for work the next morning. But the discussion kept us until midnight.

A week before, in a neighboring town about thirty miles away, between 700 and 800 people had been dragged into the street and slaughtered, and their houses and churches had been torched. The Muslims were acting on their vow to reduce the Christian population of the country to a "negligible minority."

Our discussion that night was on the question, What should

our response be as Christians when the Muslims come to our houses to do the same? It was not a theoretical question.

Satan is the father of such evil, and he has the space to kill and destroy within the dominion God assigned to man back there in the very beginning.

Satan works. He takes initiative. He has people at his disposal who will do his bidding. He has demonic forces under his command. And we can expect to be on the receiving end of his schemes.[16]

UNDERSTANDING SUFFERING AND ADVERSITY

We have identified five sources of suffering and adversity: sin, bad judgment, the laws of nature, unjust or unwise governments, and Satan. So it is not right whenever something—good or bad—happens to automatically conclude that God did it. It is also out of place to assume that everything that happens to us is "God's will." That attitude tends toward fatalism. Both man and Satan become not much more than pawns in God's game when we carry that view on out to its conclusions.

We still have not worked our way through all the tough questions this subject raises. I still have two left on my list. You may have more. Mine are:

- Is God ever the cause of suffering and adversity?
- What can I expect from God while I'm in the midst of suffering caused by these five sources we have identified?

Does God Cause Suffering and Adversity?
What about God? Does He bring about suffering? That's an exceedingly difficult question, and I don't have the answer. But I do know God uses it.

The Old Testament is filled with accounts of how God brought things into the lives of individuals and nations to accomplish His purposes with them. In the last chapter we saw how He used Assyria to turn Manasseh around.

There is no question that God allows painful things to come into our lives. Hebrews 12 is a basic passage on this subject. It teaches that God uses painful experiences as a form of parental discipline. They are actually an expression of God's love for us, and proof of our membership in His family. The writer says, "Endure hardship as discipline; God is treating you as sons. For what son is not disciplined by his father? . . . God disciplines us for our good, that we may share in his holiness."[17]

I think the origin of a particular trial that a Christian goes through is really a moot point. It doesn't make any practical difference whether God initiated it, or whether we got into it by our own wrong judgment, or whether it's the result of Satan's initiative. Since we are God's children, He takes it all, whatever the source, and uses it for His purposes.

The Cross is the great example here. It was "wicked men" inspired by Satan himself that put the Son of God on the cross.[18] This most grotesque sin in all of human history was used by God as the pivotal point for the greatest good, for all eternity.

He extends this same principle to us. "In all things God works for the good of those who love him."[19] Whatever gets dumped into our lives, whatever the source, whether it is bitter or sweet, God can make artful use of it as He makes us over to look like His Son. This moves us on to our second question.

What Can I Expect From God While I'm in the Midst of Suffering and Adversity?

We already have a partial answer to this question. God uses difficulties, from whatever source, to accomplish His purposes in us and through us. We just need to remember one thing: We do not always come out "winners" from these trials. We won't necessarily end up healthier, wealthier, and more comfortable. We will end up stronger and wiser—when we respond properly. But among the heroes in faith's "Hall of Fame" in Hebrews 11, we find people who were tortured, jeered at, flogged, chained, and imprisoned. Some were stoned, sawed in two, and killed by the sword. They wandered about destitute and mistreated, living in caves and holes in the ground. These were among the "heroes"![20]

Life, for them, did not end with a comfortable retirement.

God does not promise that He will make our sufferings go away. What He does promise is that He will be right in there with us, inseparable from us, giving us everything we need to win out over the evil, even while we are, by human standards, losing.[21]

In the next chapter we will deal with the question, How are we to handle suffering and adversity? What is the appropriate response that will leave us stronger rather than disheartened and weakened?

QUESTIONS FOR THOUGHT

1. What is your image of God? When you think of God, what descriptive words come to your mind? Write down your answers.

2. Take an objective look at your answers. How accurate do you think they are? How complete? What influenced you to answer as you did? What are your sources?

3. How would one proceed to get a more complete, more accurate understanding of who God is?

NOTES
1. 1 Corinthians 13:12.
2. Colossians 1:10.
3. Isaiah 24:4-6.
4. John 12:31.
5. Revelation 12:10-12.
6. John 12:31.
7. Luke 22:31.
8. Psalm 37:8-10.
9. Habbakuk 2:6-8.
10. Psalm 2.
11. Daniel 7:17-18.
12. 1 Corinthians 15:24.
13. Proverbs 13:13.
14. John 13:2.
15. John 13:27.

16. Ephesians 6:11-12.
17. Hebrews 12:7-10.
18. Acts 2:23; John 13:2,27.
19. Romans 8:28.
20. Hebrews 11:35-38.
21. Romans 8:31-39.

CHAPTER 10

Dealing with Suffering and Adversity

Many pressures and insecurities accompany modernity. People find themselves in debt, insecure in their employment, with their long-range financial stability at risk. Scarcity of time is a constant frustration. Relationships within the family tend to suffer as the general tempo of life escalates. When family breakup becomes a real threat, the kids react to the insecurity with behavior that makes the parents worry all the more. The scenario goes on and on, but the primary message is clear: Life today is fragile and precarious.

Peggy Noonan summarizes, "I think the essential daily predicament of modern, intelligent, early-middle-age Americans— the boomers, the basketball in the python—is this: There is no margin for error anymore. Everything has to continue as it is for us to continue with the comfort we have. And we do not believe that everything will continue as it is."[1]

Modernity brings its own spectrum of sufferings and adversities. We discussed some typical pressures in the early chapters

137

of this book. Those pressures need to be included in our conversations on suffering and adversity because they are so common among us. We who follow Christ experience our share of these pressures, and as insiders, we find ourselves surrounded by people who are struggling with their own private desperation. Most of the time you would never guess it because they live by the unwritten code, "Don't let 'em see you sweat." The pressure's always on because society turns cannibal against anyone who goes down.

The questions now are: How should we who are Christians deal with adversity as it invades our own lives? What is a proper response? Then we need to ask, How should we relate to others in their suffering?

RESPONDING TO SUFFERING AND ADVERSITY IN OUR OWN LIVES

Consider it pure joy, my brothers, whenever you face trials of many kinds. (James 1:2)

That sounds pretty extreme, does it not? I could see being encouraged to endure trials, or to trust God in them, but to find them an occasion for joy seems a little too much. Yet this same exhortation is repeated several times in Scripture.[2]

Why are we told to welcome suffering and trials? I think it is because the attitude we assume while we're in the midst of a trial will determine how we come out of it. Trials can be dangerous to our faith. They are not fire drills. They are the real thing. We can either come out of them strengthened and more Christlike or we can emerge maimed, embittered.

It is an act of faith for us to welcome something that is truly negative and painful as it comes upon us. But such a response makes a statement. It says, "God, I don't like this at all, but I accept it as Your opportunity to participate in my life in a special way—and I'm excited about that." This positions us as expectant learners rather than as morose victims of some injustice.

Everyone suffers trials, but not everyone benefits from them. In Hebrews 12:11 we read, "Discipline . . . produces a harvest of righteousness and peace *for those who have been trained by it*" (emphasis added). Discipline doesn't always bring positive results. The results are positive only for people who will accept the training the discipline can offer. Things can go the other way. So the writer warns, "Therefore strengthen your feeble arms and weak knees. Make level paths for your feet, so that the lame may not be disabled, but rather healed."

There is always the possibility of coming out of a trial with a permanent disability. We choose our response to adversity, and the choice we make will determine what comes of us.

I heard a friend of mine, George Sanchez, use the response Cain gave after he murdered his brother, Abel, as an example of what we are saying here.[3] God approved of Abel's offering and rejected Cain's. Cain became jealous, angry, and depressed. Then the Lord gave Cain one of those nuggets of truth that serves for all of us all the time. He asked, "Why are you angry? Why is your face downcast? If you do what is right, will you not be accepted? But if you do not do what is right, sin is crouching at your door; it desires to have you, but you must master it."[4]

Rather than obeying, Cain took Abel out into a field and killed him. Life was difficult for him from that point on. A wrong attitude produced a wrong response.

A right attitude will produce a right response. A right response brings a sense of approval. It lifts our spirits. A wrong attitude has the opposite effect. Anger can get you into trouble. Sanchez diagrammed the passage:

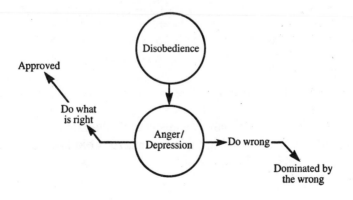

THE GOOD FRUIT OF SUFFERING AND ADVERSITY

The Fruit of Godly Character

We are reassured over and over in Scripture that trials can produce virtues in our lives that more than outweigh the pain. "We also rejoice in our sufferings, because we know that suffering produces perseverance; perseverance, character; and character, hope."[5] And, "You know that the testing of your faith develops perseverance. Perseverance must finish its work so that you may be mature and complete, not lacking anything."[6]

These and similar passages tell us there is a cause-effect relationship between our suffering and the development of a mature, godly character.

Our oldest daughter, Michelle, and her husband, Glenn, are planning on a career in missions. As a part of their preparation they moved to Baltimore so that Glenn could do a master's degree program in his field at the University of Maryland. As they uprooted themselves from their home and families and moved across the country, my wife and I prayed for them. We told God that since they were planning to spend their lives on the other side of the world, it would be important for them to have an accurate understanding of who He is so that they would have the confidence they needed to take on the future. We thought, of course, that in response to this request God would show them how trustworthy He is by meeting their needs in ways that would be unmistakably His.

We prayed. But the more we prayed, the more difficult things became for them. The only positive part of their experience was in the quality of the course Glenn was taking. Nothing else went according to their expectations, or ours. Our daughter couldn't find a job in her profession of dentistry, so she had to take a job at slightly over minimum wage as a sales clerk. Both of them had to live on her income. Housing had to be cheap, so they decided to share a little house with a couple from Asia. There were vast differences in living habits, especially in the kitchen. Then one day Michelle was driving their cantankerous old Honda and was hit from behind. The car was totaled and she suffered neck and back injuries.

As my wife and I watched all this from the sidelines, we began to go into a crisis of our own with God. He had not paid attention to our prayers, which by that time had become strident. Everything they had was gone. They were hurting and confused. And I was convinced that they wouldn't trust God enough after all this to follow Him around the block!

What we couldn't see was that God *was* answering our prayers for them. In their pain and confusion, like countless sufferers before them, they went to the book of Job. There they uncovered some longstanding inner needs that they were hardly aware of. They also saw that Job didn't understand what was happening to him either yet he never showed any resentment. His attitude was, "Though he slay me, yet will I hope in him."[7] "God was pleased with Job," they told me, "because of his character. He was proud of Job." Their conclusion was, "It all boils down to one word: trust. We are going to trust God the way Job did."

Once they had gotten past this basic decision, the door was opened for God's blessing. They have gone on to other things—other trials—in this school of faith that is our lives.

In chapter 8 we talked about the place of humility in the process of transformation. The story I have just told illustrates what was said there. Experiences take us to the Scriptures. We struggle with our attitudes in the midst of the experiences, and then comes the insight. We understand, and anyone who understands humbles himself before God. When Isaiah saw himself in contrast to God's glory he cried, "Woe to me! I am ruined!"[8] Ezekiel's reaction was identical,[9] as was the Apostle John's.[10]

Trials reveal to us things about God and about ourselves that we would have no way of seeing in any other way. Just a glimpse is enough to bring us to our knees. It breaks us of our self-satisfaction and we discover that we still have a long way to go, that there is still so much to learn. We become learners—*disciples*. We choose to persevere. "Suffering produces perseverance; perseverance, *character*."[11] We become people God can entrust with responsibility.

We like the outcome but we don't like the route that takes us there. Isn't there a more benign way? No there isn't! So we embrace suffering and adversity because they are a means God uses to transform our character and make us fit for His service.

We Glorify God Through Suffering and Adversity

We saw in chapter 2 that the insider is called to glorify God in the arena of his everyday life. To glorify, we saw, is to reveal something about God so that people can see Him more clearly. The insider reveals Christ to those around him by reflecting Christlikeness in the midst of the routines of everyday life. This is really our initial means of communication: incarnating the truth by living it out. This incarnation prepares the way for what we have to say about Christ. In the book *Living Proof*, we observed in the Epistles that, without exception, this is the sequence of communication for the insider among unbelievers. "But in your hearts set apart Christ as Lord. Always be prepared to give an answer to everyone who asks you to give the reason for the hope that you have."[12] It is the statement of the life made clear by our testimony.

It should probably not come as a surprise, then, that "suffering" and "glory" are frequently found together in Scripture.

Jesus tied them together just before He was arrested, as He explained to His disciples what was about to happen to Him. He said, "It was for this very reason I came to this hour. Father, glorify your name!"[13] The sufferings of the Cross revealed things about the Father that we could never, ever have understood in any other way.

Peter encouraged the Jewish believers who were scattered and persecuted by Nero by saying, "Rejoice that you participate in the sufferings of Christ so that you may be overjoyed when his glory is revealed." In the future, God's glory will be fully revealed. For now, Peter explains, if you are insulted, if you suffer as a Christian, do not be ashamed but praise God that you bear that name.[14] The world watches as we who bear Christ's name handle adversity. What they see can be the most powerful statement to truth that we can possibly make.

I have a friend who found himself in the middle of a very difficult business deal. Though he was innocent of any wrongdoing, the circumstances were such that he could have been implicated.

This friend was a very new Christian at the time. He was preparing to travel to meet with the other parties in the deal to attempt to resolve misunderstandings when he told me what he was facing. We turned to Philippians 4:6-7 and read it together, "Do not be anxious about anything, but in everything, by prayer . . . present your requests to God. And the peace of God . . . will guard your hearts and your minds in Christ Jesus."

We agreed to pray according to this promise, and see what God would do.

On the plane he was seated next to a business associate. At one point, this colleague, commiserating with his friend, said, "You must be nervous about all this." My friend replied, "No, I'm really not." To this associate's astonishment, my friend pulled his Bible out of his briefcase and showed him the verse we were praying over. The companion couldn't believe it. He hadn't touched a Bible in years and did not know about my friend's new faith. But it was what he saw in the man himself that captured him. He was looking at a burning bush that should have been consumed, but it wasn't. Now the two men study the Bible together. That is what it means to glorify God!

Whatever difficulty or adversity we may go through constitutes an opportunity for God to reveal something of Himself to the world. He does His work in us, comforting and strengthening us, and that shows through. People see it and realize that there is something there that does not compute with normal behavior. They have to get closer to take a better look.

We Gain Intimacy with Christ Through Suffering and Adversity

We have seen how trials can produce the good fruit of godly character, and we have seen that through them God reveals Himself in us. A third fruit of adversity is intimacy with Christ. Paul penned the words, "I want to know Christ and the power of his resurrection and the fellowship of sharing in his sufferings, becoming like him in his death, and so, somehow to attain to the resurrection from the dead."[15]

That's a strange phrase: "to attain to the resurrection of the dead." Is Paul saying he was striving to qualify for the resurrection? Hardly! That would contradict everything he understood about God's grace.

I think that what he means here is that he wants to go so deep in his fellowship with Christ that he relives all that Christ experienced. This includes experiencing Christ's resurrection power, His sufferings, and His death. The effect of such intimate identification would be post-resurrection perfection! In effect Paul is saying, "I want to become so much like Christ, share in His perfection to such an extent, that no further changes will need to be made in me on the day I find myself standing in God's presence." The next verse supports this idea, as Paul continues, "Not that I have already obtained all this, or have already been made perfect, but I press on."[16] "That's what I'm going for," he is saying.

As we give up our own comfort to serve others, as we accept being excluded from certain social circles or ridiculed by our college professors because we bear Christ's name, as we grieve over the indifference of family members and people we love—we taste a bit of what Christ suffered. History is filled with stories of people who laid down their lives for their faith. Martyrdom and imprisonment because of Christ is common in our generation. But there is more than one way to lay down one's life for Christ. We are all, in fact, called to this.[17] The reward is a deepened relationship with Christ.

RESPONDING TO SUFFERING AND ADVERSITY IN THE LIVES OF OTHERS

We get the news. A friend has been in an accident and is in the hospital. A neighbor's child is on drugs and is in trouble with the law. A friend's marriage is on the verge of breaking up. Another friend was laid off from work and there are bills to pay. Alcoholism is out of control in someone's life.

News of this nature comes to us almost daily. We are saddened, and feel helpless. We might stop what we're doing and pray for the situation. Occasionally we'll visit someone in the hospital.

Or we might call the pastor and ask him to go visit. Isn't that his job? Beyond that what else can we do?

Our helplessness leaves us feeling guilty. We withdraw from the scene and busy ourselves with our own affairs. It's hard to be around people with needs when you can't do anything to help. The effect of our feelings of awkwardness is that people who are suffering find themselves alone and on their own precisely at the time when they need help the most.

Being alone when you are in crisis, to know you have no one to turn to, that it's up to *you*, can be as difficult as the crisis itself.

What is a proper response on our part?

"IF ONE PART SUFFERS, EVERY PART SUFFERS"[18]

These words from 1 Corinthians 12 supply the basic principle upon which our response to suffering and adversity needs to be established. Together, we who are Christ's are a body. As such, we all need one another all the time. We need one another to keep ourselves moving toward a healthy, godly lifestyle. We need each other to fill in the gaps in our efforts as insiders. And we certainly need one another when we're hurting.

If you stub your toe and break it, the rest of your body doesn't go on about its business as if it didn't happen. That toe stops everything else that is going on and becomes the center of attention until it gets fixed. When someone within the body of Christ suffers adversity, it is an opportunity for us to demonstrate what community is really all about. More than that—what the *gospel* is all about.

A couple years ago, my wife and I revisited our friends in Brazil, with whom we had spent many years of our lives. The ties between us are strong, for many of them are our spiritual offspring. We had read about the escalating inflation in the economy and were wondering what kind of hardship it was causing among our friends. In reply to our questions on the subject, one person explained that the situation was actually working to the advantage of the gospel. He went on to illustrate.

Eduardo, a mature Christian and owner of a small business, found himself caught in an unpredictable inflationary swing. He was suddenly insolvent and headed for bankruptcy. Paulo, a relatively new Christian Eduardo had been helping to follow Christ, got wind of the situation. He took Eduardo out for lunch and got him to list all of his debts. When they were all down on paper, Paulo said, "We're going to take care of these for you." And they did.

The friend who told us this story went on to explain that unbelievers who had observed this and similar situations among the Christians are "getting in line to study the Bible with us."

Short on *Words*, Long on *Service*

A few years ago, one of my colleagues lost a son. He was shot in a random killing. This colleague is part of a four-man support and accountability group. When the other three got the news, they immediately dropped everything. They and their wives flew to our city to come to the aid of this colleague, his wife, and their children. I watched in amazement as those three couples simply took over. They ran the house, made the arrangements, handled the press, the guests, and on and on. My colleague and his wife, stricken with grief, found themselves surrounded with support. They didn't need words of consolation. What, in such circumstances, can you say anyway? They needed to be served, and that's what they got.

What is there to say to a widow when she walks back into her house after burying her husband? What do you say to the friend who has just lost his job, while the bills keep coming? It is usually safe, at these times, to be short on words and long on service. Most of us are not qualified to say much, so the more we try, the more we sound like Job's friends.

We've all observed, I'm sure, how a person who is suffering a particular trial will gravitate toward another who has been through something similar. I have not lost my mate, nor any of our children. There are many forms of suffering I have never experienced, but I have experienced suffering in some areas. In those areas where I have suffered, I might have some words that can help—occasionally. But just because we haven't been there ourselves doesn't mean we cannot serve significantly. Service can take many forms. There is one service that eclipses all the rest.

The Service of Intercession

"I'll be praying for you." We hear those words often. Sometimes we use them ourselves. They can either be a glib, noncommittal way of expressing our support for a Christian in need, or they can be a statement of commitment and of sacrifice for someone. I have used this statement in both ways, and when I catch myself using it glibly I am forced to acknowledge my hypocrisy. An offer to pray, to seriously intercede, is no consolation prize. It is the first prize.

Herod arrested the Apostle James and executed him. When he saw that his approval went up with the Jews, he set out to do the same to Peter. He arrested him, too, and put him in prison to await his turn. The account proceeds, "But the church was earnestly praying to God for him."[19] The text sounds like James would have lived, too, had the same thing been done for him.

We referred earlier to Paul's close call with death. He explains his escape by saying, "On [God] we have set our hope that he will continue to deliver us, as you help us by your prayers."[20] James writes, "The prayer of a righteous man is powerful and effective."[21]

I have a manageable number of prayer commitments that I keep in my Bible next to my Bible reading page. They are a serious part of my life. Through prayer I participate in other people's lives. Some are neighbors, some live in other cities, others on other continents. But these commitments keep us close. I make it a point to keep current, updating the news on what is happening at every opportunity, if not face-to-face, then by telephone.

It is a struggle to participate in someone else's suffering through prayer. You go through the same fears and doubts that that person does. His or her struggle becomes your struggle. He or she soon senses that, and takes courage from it. He or she knows he or she is not alone. And God answers. Over and over again I have seen needs met and crises resolved in ways that leave God's imprint clear.

This is a two-way street. The people for whom you actively pray will often pray for you in the same fashion.

This subject of prayer brings closure to our entire discussion on suffering and adversity.

OVERCOMING SUFFERING AND ADVERSITY THROUGH FAITH

For everyone born of God has overcome the world.
This is the victory that has overcome the world, even our faith.[22]

We have seen how God has given man his own space, his own dominion, and how Satan has preempted it. Together, man and Satan have transformed life into an ordeal for most of humanity. The Cross and the resurrection broke Satan's control, so we who belong to Christ are freed from his dominion. In Christ, we have the authority to overcome him.

The source of our suffering or adversity really doesn't make any difference. It can come from our own waywardness, from the sins of others, or from Satan himself. All authority in heaven and on earth has been given to Christ,[23] so whatever the source, Christ has overcome it. On that basis we can, by faith and through prayer, bring our needs to God. As we do so, we can be confident that He will respond. Sometimes He responds by turning our circumstances around; sometimes He responds by turning our hearts around—giving us the grace to endure.

We need the long view. God's people must suffer like everyone else. In order to see what we're really made of, we may have to be placed under incredible pressure. But that may be the only way we'll ever recognize that God's grace is real. The long view says, "I consider that our present sufferings are not worth comparing with the glory that will be revealed in us."[24]

Our perspective on history needs to be the same. Habakkuk struggled with the issue of God's involvement, or apparent noninvolvement, in the sufferings of his people, Judah. Take twenty minutes and read the book for yourself. Observe the dialogue between Habakkuk and God. Is it not the same as what we have carried on in these two chapters?

In the midst of the dialogue, God reassures Habakkuk. He tells him that Judah's enemies "exhaust themselves for nothing," and that "the earth will be filled with the knowledge of the glory of the LORD, as the waters cover the sea."[25] To visualize what we have been saying:

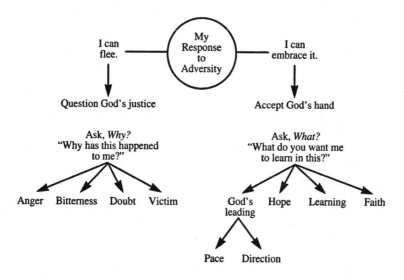

Ministering When Others Experience Suffering and Adversity

1. Demonstrate love and commitment by taking the time to communicate your awareness of their situation and their needs.

2. Refrain from giving your advice. Rather, mourn with those who mourn. Silent service is always safe. Otherwise you could become like one of Job's friends!

3. Avoid over-spiritualizing and help others avoid it. Refrain from saying, "God told me to tell you . . ." even if it seems that God did. By making that statement you elevate the authority of your words to where they are beyond dispute.

4. Help people recognize that adversity can come from many sources. Help them focus on how to respond rather than on attaching blame or criticizing external circumstances.

5. When we suffer, it is an opportunity for us to be transparent with our sisters and brothers. When they suffer, it's an opportunity to practice community.

6. Trials are dangerous. They can discourage and dishearten. This opens the way for Satan to cause permanent damage, such as bitterness. We must pray for people in trials and encourage them.

NOTES

1. Peggy Noonan, "You'd Cry Too If It Happened to You, *Forbes* (September 14, 1992), vol. 150, number 6, page 64.
2. Romans 5:3, 1 Peter 1:6-7, 4:12-19.
3. See Genesis 4:1-7.
4. Genesis 4:6-7.
5. Romans 5:3-4.
6. James 1:3-4.
7. Job 13:15.
8. Isaiah 6:5.
9. Ezekiel 1:28.
10. Revelation 1:17.
11. Romans 5:3.
12. 1 Peter 3:15.
13. John 12:27.
14. 1 Peter 4:13-16.
15. Philippians 3:10.
16. Philippians 3:12.
17. Luke 9:23-24.
18. 1 Corinthians 12:26.
19. Acts 12:5.
20. 2 Corinthians 1:10-11.
21. James 5:16.
22. 1 John 5:4-5.
23. Matthew 28:18.
24. Romans 8:18.
25. Habakkuk 2:13-14.

CHAPTER 11

Competence as Insiders

L et's review our train of thought to this point to make sure
we have our bearings on where we've been and where we
need to go from here.

We began by talking about modernity, the mind-set or way
of thinking that modern life imposes on us. With modernity our
beliefs tend to become relative and our sense of belonging tentative. The basis for accountability for behavior is lost. As a result,
society loses its way and people are damaged.

The effects of modernity are also evident in our churches. We
see those effects in the way we relate to one another, in our
definitions of success, and in our basic understanding of what
the church is all about. Too often there isn't that much difference between the Christian and the unbeliever in the way we
live our lives. Consequently, our uniqueness as God's people
wanes, and with that goes our effect as seasoning in society.
Modernity is redrawing the map both within the church and
without.

Traditionally we have assumed we can discharge our responsibilities to the unbelievers by somehow attracting them to come into our churches. A certain percentage will come, but it is obvious that the mainstream will pass us by. This heightens the importance of the person we are calling the "insider." Insiders are Christians who see a person's everyday arena of life as the logical place of ministry. The sets of relationships that are unique to us should be our God-given arena of service.

Our goal as insiders is to help people know Christ and to experience the healing and transformation He provides. This involves helping a person take his first steps—and then keep on walking toward spiritual maturity. The ministry of insiders could be described as spiritual parenthood.

This walk toward maturity goes through a battlefield. And it goes on throughout one's lifetime. In fact, the insider soon discovers there really isn't that much difference between where he or she is on the road to maturity and where the people he or she is reaching out to actually find themselves. It is the same road. The goals and needs are similar. Both must deal with old, entrenched habit patterns and both will spend their lives being transformed into the image of Christ. These things do not come without struggle.

When we become involved in other people's lives, we soon discover that they too are suffering. Suffering is inescapable. It comes in many forms, from a variety of sources. It ranges from calamitous events that permanently alter our lives to the daily distress brought on by the pressures of modern life. Suffering can either forge strong character or permanently debilitate. It promises great gain, and threatens great loss. The outcome depends on our response. As insiders, we need to understand suffering, deal with it in our own lives for God's glory, and know how to serve others who are in the middle of it.

As this description of insiders and of the scope of our responsibilities grows, it becomes apparent that what we are talking about is at the heart of what the church should be all about. The church is a people gathered unto Christ and sent into the world. In this book we are describing part of what that sending entails.

If insiders are indeed central to God's purposes for the

church, then it follows that our needs for being equipped and resourced deserve the highest priority. If we are going to make it, we need support from the rest of the body and from our leaders. I describe the nature of this support in *Church Without Walls*.

We now need to organize all of these things we have discussed into manageable categories. This will allow us, as insiders, to organize our own thinking as we proceed to minister to others. Questions abound at this point. We probably feel insecure and uncertain about our ability to do the things we've talked about. Where, I ask, do I begin? How should I go about it? What should I be aiming for?

There are usually too many variables to successfully transfer methods that have worked for one person to another situation. So we will address these questions by describing three tracks that should get us there. We identified these three tracks in chapter 4. They are *community*, *competence*, and *character*. In this chapter we will explore each of these more thoroughly.

Our discussion is intended to serve a double purpose. It should help us, as insiders, to stay on track in our own lives and ministries, and it will also help us know the route to take with others.

COMMUNITY

No one gets very far in his or her progress toward spiritual maturity without community. Growth does not happen in a vacuum. Look through the Epistles and observe how much of the content has to do with Christians relating to one another. We are told to be devoted to one another, to serve one another, to bear with one another in love, to share with those in need, to forgive each other, to look not only after one's own interests but also the interests of others, and more. The ultimate was penned by the Apostle John when he said, "This is how we know what love is: Jesus Christ laid down his life for us. And we ought to lay down our lives for our brothers."[1]

The implications are obvious. If we don't have community, we really have no context to put these instructions into practice.

And if we can't practice them, we can't grow in them. Our spiritual development will be stunted.

Community: A Living Bond

The dictionary defines community as "a group of people living together as a smaller social unit within a larger one, and having interests, work, etc., in common."[2] Usage of the word is so broad that if you are a human being, you are inescapably included in communities several times over. You are a part of a community if you are a church member. Wherever you might live—on a farm, in a town, or in a section of a city—you are a part of that community. We now talk about the European community, and even the global community.

When we use the word community here, we mean a lot more than any of these usages imply. When the New Testament talks about our relationship with one another, it assumes commitment and action. It is more than membership in a social structure. The Apostle John gets to the essence of community as we are using the word:

> We proclaim to you what we have seen and heard, so that
> you may have fellowship with us. And our fellowship is
> with the father and with his son, Jesus Christ. . . . God is
> light; in him there is no darkness at all. If we claim to have
> fellowship with him yet walk in the darkness, we lie and
> do not live by the truth. But if we walk in the light, as he is
> in the light, we have fellowship with one another, and the
> blood of Jesus, his Son, purifies us from all sin.[3]

There are three key phrases in this passage: *fellowship, walking in the light*, and *walking in darkness*. All three contribute to our understanding of what it means to be in community as God's people.

The word *fellowship* describes what should go on between ourselves and God, and between one another. It means a "living bond," or "mutual abiding."[4]

What does it mean to have a living bond with another person?

Jesus modeled the answer to this question in the way He related to His Father. He said, "The Son can do nothing by himself; he can do only what he sees his Father doing, because whatever the Father does, the Son also does. For the Father loves the Son and shows him all he does."

Jesus lived in dependence on His Father, and the Father depended on His Son. Thus God accomplished His purposes through His Son. Near the end of His life, Jesus said to His Father, "I have brought glory on earth by completing the work you gave me to do."[5]

A living bond is a two-way street of interdependence between parties, in this case between the Father and His Son.

Amazingly, Jesus went on to extend an invitation to us to participate in this same intimacy with Him and with His Father! Jesus prayed "that they may be one as we are one: I in them and you in me. May they be brought to complete unity to let the world know that you sent me and have loved them even as you have loved me."[6] If this is Christ's desire for us, if He has opened the possibility of such a relationship for us, only a fool would not pursue entering into it with all his heart. We enter into this intimacy by *walking in the light.*

Remember, "God is light; in him there is no darkness at all."[7] If we are to walk with Him, we will have to step into the light. That is a frightening thought. We don't mind stepping into the light to show off the good that is in us. It's the *bad* that keeps us hiding in the shadows. We feel ashamed and afraid; we shrink away from God's invitation. We fear exposure. We're like Adam and Eve hiding behind some leaves in the garden. But who are we kidding? We might just as well step out into the open before God because He already knows exactly where we are and what we're up to.

To walk in the light means to bring our deeds, both good and bad, into God's presence. It is not perfection. Rather, it is an admission of imperfection. It's getting what we *are* out into the open so that God can do His work in us.

A synonym for "walking in the light" is "living by the truth." (See also John 3:21.) Walking in the light implies a certain attitude on my part toward truth. Truth is not just a matter of having sound doctrine or of being right in one's interpretation of Scripture. Important as that is, it is secondary to seeking God's truth for the sake of personal transformation.

It is possible to have right doctrine, to be able to defend the truth against all challengers, and yet walk in darkness at the same time. Where one's attitude is wrong, "truth" can become the center of conflict and division.

I once happened upon a tiny brick church building in an old part of a city in England. It had been built before the turn of the century. The name of the church explained its tiny size. It was "The Correct Baptist Church." If the prevailing question in our fellowship is which of us is correct, you and I will soon find ourselves in trouble with each other. Eventually we will part company—and one of us will get to keep the building. And so we will go on to repeat the process. We will have totally misunderstood God's purpose in His giving us access to truth. The primary purpose of truth is to lead us into a living bond with God Himself, with His Son, and with one another.

I cannot have such a bond with you if I do not have one with God. What is the connection between the two?

It is helpful to look at the third key phrase in 1 John 1 to gain the answer to this question. It is "walk in darkness."[8] *Walking in darkness means persisting in wrong behavior. It is refusing to bring the lies that control our lives into the light of God's truth.*

If I am hiding in the dark from God, not being open before Him about the things that are going on, you can be sure I'll try to keep you in the dark as well. I might attend the meetings, participate in the discussions, and go through the other motions, but nothing of importance will happen. That is because I will try to keep a similar distance between you and me to what I maintain between myself and God.

In this manner, it is easy for a person's progress toward maturity to come to an impasse. Rebellion or fear can keep me lurking in the shadows in my relationship with God, and consequently with my brothers and sisters as well. Something has to give if I am to move ahead. The breakthrough can happen either in my interactions with God or while I'm with others. For me, it has most often happened while I'm with others. That's because fellowship with one another, as we've been describing it here, has a tremendous power. It can gently pry us out of our dark seclusion and bring us into light and truth. I think that is why the paragraph in this passage ends with the phrase, "And the blood of Jesus, his Son, purifies us from every sin."[9] This purification happens in the context of the living bond we have with one another—as the outgrowth of our fellowship with God. There is a good reason for that.

Community: A Safe Place for Transformation

It is safe to walk with one another in the light. Where there is light, things are clear and out in the open. But it is treacherous to try to walk in the darkness with others.

I have been in Christian communities where I have felt unsafe. I'm sure most of us have. I feel unsafe where there seems to be an unspoken agreement in the group that nothing unpredictable will be said by anyone, or where everything is always just right and everyone seems to be getting along wonderfully all the time. Then there are the situations where I get the impression that the others are just waiting for me to say something wrong. Judgment seems to prowl in these circles. And there are the situations where I know that if I say anything worthy of gossip, it will be snatched up. The prudent thing to do in any of these situations is for me to keep things to myself.

But I need a place where it's safe to bring things into the light if I am to continue to grow. So do the other people in my life who have the same desires. We all need an environment where we can talk openly about the things we're thinking about, the things that are going on in our lives, without fear of being rejected, gossiped about, or judged. We need people who love us enough to be honest with us, who will help us stay in the truth.

I am not suggesting that we must confess our sins to one another. There are certain times and sins for which this is quite appropriate. But often it is not. I am saying we need to be trans-parent. That means we stop being defensive, that we be ready to listen to one another and receive the exhortations of others. This is very, very difficult for some people. We must gently earn the transparency of others.

Transparency is earned as we practice speaking the truth in love. Ephesians 4:15 says that as we "speak the truth in love, we will in all things grow up into him." Truth and love must work together if there is to be growth. Truth can become a lethal weapon in the hands of a person who does not love. Love dictates the dosage and the timing of the truth we share with someone else. But if we truly love others, we will speak the truth to that person. Not to do so would be a form of betrayal. So the two—truth and love—must go together. And when they do, we become safe to others.

There is great power in being a safe place for others. Over and over I have watched people experience deliverance and freedom from all sorts of bondage as they open up before God in the company of their brothers and sisters. Often this happens as we talk about how to pray for one another, and then also as we go to God in prayer together.

But sharing with one another in the name of transparency and truthfulness can be easily perverted. When truthfulness is sharpened into a weapon, it can do serious damage. But when it is used with love, it can be used to help cure. We can be indiscreet in the things we share. The best protection against this, beyond the things we have already said, is to be careful about the *kind* of truth our conversations revolve around. We can never disconnect from God's truth. The Scriptures must be our frame of reference at all times.

Community: The Insider's Vehicle for Ministry

One of the most common failures of people I know who seek to labor as insiders is that they attempt to go it alone. They may belong to a church and have many Christian friends, yet when it comes to pursuing their calling as insiders they are really on their own. They have no vehicle, no kindred spirits to accompany them, to help them get to where they want to go.

In the American culture we were raised to believe we can do

almost anything on our own. So, we set off alone on this venture as well, unaware that something essential is missing. Over and over again I have watched people set out to labor as insiders with great expectations of fruitfulness, only to emerge years later frustrated over the fact that very little has happened. Often they still do not understand that their problems stem, at least in part, from their individualism.

We were not made to go it alone. God gave each of us some gifts and He withheld others. We have some time at our disposal, but not enough. We have a little experience in a few things, but we lack in many areas. We are deficient by God's design. We need our deficiencies because without them we wouldn't need one another. Power resides in oneness. Jesus prayed "that all of them may be one, Father," and "May they also be in us so that the world may believe that you have sent me."[10]

The Power of Community in Ministry

There are two reasons why we need one another as we minister. First, we need access to the gifts and abilities that we do not possess in ourselves. In addition, the power of our witness to the gospel needs to be amplified as we live it out together among our unbelieving friends.

In a secular community we find tradesmen, bankers, farmers, manufacturers, professionals, homemakers, and so on. Each is occupied with his or her particular service, but by cooperating together, everyone has all they need. Community implies doing more than just meeting together. It is also working together. It looks more like Main Street than it does an assembly hall.

The little community, the safe place we have been describing, can often serve a second, equally important function for the insider. It can also be our vehicle for ministry. A ministry vehicle is a nucleus of two or three couples and/or singles of like mind who have decided to work together among their unbelieving neighbors, social acquaintances, and families.

Over the past few years my wife and I, together with our almost out-of-the-nest children, have served as such a vehicle for one another. Our children have friends who become curious about the gospel as they observe their lives. They often bring these friends to the house for a weekend. There they see more, and somewhere over the weekend the conversations will drift toward the Scriptures. That's almost inevitable since Christ is the only cogent explanation for what makes our family tick. Sometimes we will do an initial Bible study with them. Soon these friends become interested in looking into the Scriptures with our children to understand more about Christ. Our children are comfortable teaming up with us in this way because they know we will not "dump the truck" on their friends. They know it's safe, that we will help and not drive their friends off.

In a similar way, our children help us with our unbelieving friends. They take an interest in them. And when they come over, our children will sit and talk with them. The subject matter of the conversations is irrelevant, because it's the attitudes and values that are going to be transmitted, whatever the topic. In this society where children's "games" often have fatal consequences, parents are almost frantic for help. Our children give them hope. Thus they help us move ahead with the gospel among our friends.

Teamwork of this sort can assume all sorts of variations. It requires some creative thinking and some trial and error to achieve teamwork, but when you have it, ministering to others not only becomes possible—it becomes fun. Thus, the living bond that is community serves us, not only in the transformation of our inner persons but also in the accomplishing of our calling to minister as insiders.

COMPETENCE

Competence, our second track toward spiritual maturity, has to do with the knowledge and skills we need in order to labor as insiders. Most people feel incompetent. Many are paralyzed by their feelings of incompetence. The whole idea of helping someone grow in Christ seems so daunting that we often opt for a solution that we know is ill fitting. Yet we do it. When an acquaintance shows interest, we simply invite him or her to attend church with us. So our friends remain unreached, and we remain in our incompetence.

The problem of incompetence is real. Most of us lack competence and we don't know where to turn to get it.

Years ago, when I was getting started in sharing my faith and in helping people grow, I felt so inadequate that I found myself hoping my friends wouldn't show up for our appointments. I had no idea what to do with them. I felt awkward and uncomfortable and wanted to give up. One day it occurred to me that here I was studying at the university to prepare myself for a career. I was willing to invest seven years and all the money I had to get an education so that I could earn a living. I was also spending hours every week working on my skills as an artist. And I liked sports. I would think nothing of spending time working at improving in one sport or another. It occurred to me that I would not become skilled with the gospel without similar dedication and concentrated effort.

So, I had an idea. I knew of three other friends who were in the same boat. I talked to them and we came up with a plan. We gave ourselves an initial assignment. It was to answer the question, What does a person need to be, know, and do if he is to thrive in his Christian life? We recognized that our lists could be endless, so we restricted ourselves to twenty items each. We met and combined our work.

Our plan was to agree on a topic and then go to the Scriptures individually to see what they had to say about it. We met every two weeks to compare notes and learn from one another until we had worked through the list.

It did not take very many months before our confidence began to grow. The Bible itself was our resource. We relied on recall, limited as it was, and a concordance to pull together what the Bible has to say on a subject. That way, we had ownership of the things we were learning. We had dug things out for ourselves.

We covered topics such as how to understand and apply the Bible in practical terms, how to pray effectively, what the gospel is and how is it communicated. We also studied how to be a spiritual parent, how to recognize needs and know how to respond to them, and so on.

One other factor contributed to the effectiveness of this effort. Most of us were at the same time involved in ministering to other people. This allowed for immediate, although I must admit often ill-fitting, applications of the things we were learning.

The purpose of this story is not to suggest that you need to put yourself through the same procedure. Rather, it is to underscore the need we all have to deliberately set out to become competent in this greatest of all enterprises. Pay the price. It will be worth it.

We came out of our experience feeling competent. Competence and confidence go hand in hand. If anything, we were overconfident. But that was okay because it resulted in action. And experience can only come from doing.

Competence in Knowledge and Skill

We need competence in two areas: knowledge and skill. To be competent as insiders there are things we need to know, and there are things we need to know how to do.

Competence in Knowledge—

Do your best to present yourself to God as one approved, a workman who does not need to be ashamed and who correctly handles the word of truth. (2 Timothy 2:15)

This instruction was written by Paul to his spiritual son and protégé, Timothy. Timothy served as an apostle, a pastor, and a teacher. Few of us will follow in Timothy's steps, but this does not diminish our need for competence in our grasp and use of the Scriptures. It is the only tool of our trade as insiders.

Mastery of the Scriptures begins with using them as our reference point for our own lives. It means reading and rereading, studying and restudying, memorizing and meditating *on the Scriptures themselves*. Other books and tapes can be helpful but they are no substitute for "the word of truth" itself.

Competence with the Scriptures is foundational to every other area of knowledge in which we need competence. The most basic of these other areas are:

- *Competence in our knowledge of the gospel.* This includes an understanding of the great truths of the gospel and of their outworking in our lives. We talked about this in chapter 3.

    We need to assume that the gospel addresses our problems and needs, even the deepest of them. That means we need to apply ourselves to connecting these truths to the issues of life, beginning with ourselves.

- *An understanding of the people we relate to.* This begins with our understanding what the Bible has to say about human nature itself. Then we need to go on from there to an understanding of how our contemporaries think, what is important to them, and what they're up against. We need this knowledge if we are to serve people with the gospel according to their needs.

- *An understanding of spiritual growth.* We need to understand the goals of discipling and what goes into the process that moves us toward those goals.

    We will not do well at discipling others if our efforts are random, or spasmodic. We need to understand that our destination is maturity in Christ. We need a vision for spiritual generations that will go on and multiply.

Competence in Know-How—Certain skills are basic to ministering as an insider. If you acquire them, they will serve you well wherever you might be. Some of these are:

- *Hospitality.* How to open your home and serve people in such a way that they are at ease with you.
- *How to be a team player.* How to key off of other people's strengths. How to network.
- *How to listen.*
- *How to awaken the interest of unbelievers in biblical truth.*
- *How to explain the gospel to an unbeliever in an*

hour.
- *How to explore the gospel with unbelievers for a year,* if necessary, and hold their interest.
- *How to be a spiritual parent.* How to recognize needs and know how to proceed to meet them.
- *How to counsel when you're not a pro.*
- *How to be a catalyst for a small group*—to bring together a right mix of people and then to keep it dynamic. Knowing when and how to divide or expand.
- *How to teach in a small-group setting*—teaching without telling. The art of asking questions.

As you review these items you will recognize the ones you need most for your situation. Some of the skills you need might be missing from this list. Together with your team, you need to think your way through your own situation, to identify those skills that are a priority. Once identified, they can be developed.

The Myth of Omni-Competence
You're probably already good at some of the things we've listed. And there are probably other things that with some effort you could do well.

No one is good at everything, and we shouldn't try to be. What God wants is for us to be good at what we're good at, and let others in His body do the rest. We all have natural abilities, and all of us have been given spiritual gifts. Both of these are from God and we need to be good stewards of them. It is not difficult to become good at things you are gifted to do, or can do naturally. But it does take practice.

This is the message of the parable of the talents.[11] It is also in Paul's instructions to the Christians in Rome where he says, "Think of yourself with sober judgment, in accordance with the measure of faith God has given you."[12] It is certainly clear in Paul's exhortation to Timothy when he said, "I remind you to fan into flame the gift of God."[13]

So we need to keep in mind that not all of these skills are required of any single individual. When we see ourselves as a body, working in community with one another, we will find that what one person lacks, another person compensates for with his strengths.

CHARACTER

Of the three tracks to spiritual maturity—*community, competence,* and *character*—character is by far the most basic. It is also the most difficult to acquire. Community can grow up almost overnight. It will take you a couple of years to become competent. But it will take you the rest of your life to develop your character. And in the end, the outcome of your life will be determined by your character.

Character is one's moral strength or constitution. It is the fortitude one has in the face of contrary influences. You are defined as a person by your character. That definition will either enhance or throw doubt upon everything you do.

As the nation of Israel was preparing to enter the land of Canaan to occupy it, God gave the people detailed instructions on how to live in that land. If they followed them, they would avoid many problems and enjoy a very high standard of living. These instructions are found in the book of Deuteronomy.

In this material we find instructions for the kings that the people eventually wanted to appoint to lead them. One set of instructions reads:

> The king, moreover, must not acquire great numbers of horses for himself or make the people return to Egypt to get more of them, for the LORD has told you, "You are not to go back that way again." He must not take many wives, or his heart will be led astray. He must not accumulate large amounts of silver and gold.
>
> When he takes the throne of his kingdom, he is to write for himself on a scroll a copy of this law, taken from that of the priests, who are Levites. It is to be with him, and he is to read it all the days of his life so that he may learn to revere the LORD his God.[14]

These instructions are intriguing. There are compelling reasons behind each of them. It is especially interesting to observe that the first action of a new king was to obtain a copy of Moses' writings (the first five books of the Bible) and make a copy for himself. Those were the days of quills and ink, one letter at a time, page after page. It must have taken months. Then the king was to read what he had copied every day from then on throughout his reign. The reasons had to do with preserving the *character* of the king. The text reads, "so that he may learn to revere the LORD his God and follow carefully all the words of this law and these decrees and not consider himself better than his brothers and turn from the law."[15]

Nothing less than the fate of the nation was at stake in these instructions. The passage continues, "Then he and his descendants will reign a long time over his kingdom in Israel."[16]

How to Blow 1,125 Years of Progress in a Decade

It took approximately 1,125 years for God to take the nation of Israel from its birth to its zenith. Abraham left Haran in pursuit of God's promises around 2085 BC. The temple in Jerusalem was finished in the year 960 BC under Solomon's reign. Solomon brought Israel to its finest hour, and to its ruin. In the latter part of Solomon's life, he got into some things that compromised his character. It was enough to bring down the nation.

As Solomon began his reign, it seemed he could do no wrong. He was brilliant and wise, yet he was humble.

Early in Solomon's reign, God came to him in a dream and said, "Ask for whatever you want me to give you."[17]

Solomon responded, "I am only a little child and do not know how to carry on my duties. Your servant is here among the people you have chosen . . . so give your servant a discerning heart to govern your people and to distinguish between right and wrong."[18]

God was pleased with Solomon and granted his request. Solomon became the wisest man that ever lived. The Bible records that Solomon became greater, wiser, and richer than all the other kings on earth. The world beat a path to his door just to listen to him.

Then it was as if he referred to that passage in Deuteronomy and set out to do the opposite. He bought horses and chariots—the horses from Egypt. He amassed gold and silver. He took many foreign women as wives and began to worship their pagan gods.

God passed sentence on Israel. The nation was divided when Solomon died, and both parts went into decline. One part, Israel, fell to Assyria in the year 723 BC and the other part, Judah, to Babylon in 586 BC.

This is a sobering, thought-provoking story. Solomon knew the Scriptures. He was wise. He started well, but he ended up being discredited because he got into things that eroded his character. The lesson in this is that we are all going to have to spend the rest of our lives tending our character. Our intelligence won't save us. Neither will our experience. Our mental gardens will always need daily weeding. If they are neglected, we are fully capable of marring or destroying the efforts of our lifetime, as well as those of others.

The Place of Character in Our Ministry as Insiders

Godly character is essential to our effectiveness as insiders because our ministry is essentially incarnational. *Incarnation* is to embody in the flesh. People need to see the gospel lived out in us if they are going to understand what it really is that we have to offer. If the quality of character is not there, the best knowledge and skills become meaningless. Our TV evangelists have the knowledge and they have honed their skills to an art form, but the notorious flaws in character of some turn it all to straw. Where there is a breakdown of character, the gospel is discredited. About such people the Bible says, "God's name is blasphemed among the Gentiles because of you."[19]

We are instructed to "live such good lives among the pagans that . . . they may see your good deeds and glorify God on the day he visits us."[20]

Growing in Character

We rejoice in our sufferings, because we know that suffering produces perseverance; perseverance, character; and character, hope.[21]

Where and how do we acquire godly character? It comes from experiences with God and His Word. It comes out of suffering. Chapters 9 and 10 are really about forging character.

We will never get to where we want to be and we will never finish well if we do not pursue godly character. Life is long and temptations abound. It takes character to persevere, to keep on going.

CONCLUSION

So community, competence, and character must work together if we are to become mature in Christ.

Community is essential to our continued progress for two basic reasons. We need a safe place where we can walk in the light of truth. And we need our sisters and brothers, with their gifts and abilities, if our efforts as insiders are to bear fruit. It takes *competence* if we hope to mature in Christ. Feelings of incompetence paralyze us; competence, on the other hand, gives us the confidence to act, to do the things that will make us experienced. Experience is an essential to maturity. As our *character* grows, our capacity to persevere and endure increases, enabling us to go right down to the end.

QUESTIONS FOR APPLICATION

1. Summarize the characteristics of community. How would you envision the formation of such a community in your situation? How would it look? How would it work?

2. In what areas do you feel the need to develop competence? To whom can you go? What can you do to gain this competence?

3. What influences threaten your character? What do you feel you need by way of encouragement and support in

order for you to make it to the finish line as a credit to
God's name?

NOTES
1. 1 John 3:16.
2. *Webster's New World Dictionary, 2nd College Edition* (New York: Simon &
   Schuster, Prentice Hall Press, 1985), page 288.
3. 1 John 1:3-7.
4. Gerhard Kittel, *Theological Dictionary of the New Testament*, vol. III (Grand
   Rapids, MI: Eerdmans, 1965), pages 807-808.
5. John 17:4.
6. John 17:22-23.
7. 1 John 1:5.
8. 1 John 1:6.
9. John 1:7.
10. John 17:21.
11. Matthew 25:14-30.
12. Romans 12:3.
13. 2 Timothy 1:6.
14. Deuteronomy 17:16-19.
15. Deuteronomy 17:19-20.
16. Deuteronomy 17:20.
17. 1 Kings 3:5.
18. 1 Kings 3:8-9.
19. Romans 2:24.
20. 1 Peter 2:12.
21. Romans 5:3.

CHAPTER 12

God's Purposes and You

God is still creating. He is actively, purposefully at work on an enterprise of cosmic proportions. The plans for the things He is doing right now were in His mind before He began the creation of this world. People are at the center of this new creation. And the purchase price for these people was the suffering of the Cross. God knew before He made anything at all what it was going to cost Him. Yet He did it.[1] Why? we ask. Things must look very different from His perspective!

We look at the world and swear that it is out of control. All we can see is injustice, violence, and pain. Greed and hatred drive our global business and political activities. Many of us had hoped that modern man with his superior education would transform the world into a kinder, safer place—but that hope has died. Increased knowledge has only made man more cunning in his evil.

The world has gone berserk and we are left, together with Habakkuk, complaining before God:

Why do you tolerate wrong?
Destruction and violence are before me;
    there is strife, and conflict abounds.
Therefore the law is paralyzed,
    and justice never prevails.
The wicked hem in the righteous,
    so that justice is perverted.[2]

God's response to Habakkuk is His response to us as well. He told Habakkuk that the things he was seeing, that had him so worked up, are like a passing summer storm. The nations are really exhausting themselves for nothing, says God. He assures Habakkuk that His eternal purposes are proceeding unaffected, unaltered. And the day will come when,

"the earth will be filled with the knowledge of the glory
        of the LORD,
    as the waters cover the sea."[3]

Empires will come and go, as will nations. Business and economic structures will be even more fleeting. The sole survivor of our age will be this enterprise that God is pursuing.

God is creating an inheritance for His Son consisting of people out of every tribe and nation in the world. These people, His church, are being adopted into God's family. They will share in all that is His. He will even *give* them the Kingdom!

Evil existed before the creation of the world, but it will have no place in the new creation. The Cross and the empty tomb not only opened the way for our reconciliation to God; they terminated Satan's rule. His current flurry of activity is really his death throes. All things, the realms we know about and those we don't, are being brought under God's dominion.[4]

God is making everything new. He is creating a new heaven and earth where even our familiar laws of physics will be useless. John writes,

"Now the dwelling of God is with men, and he will live
with them. They will be his people, and God himself
will be with them and be their God. . . . The old order of
things has passed away."

He who was seated on the throne said, "I am making
everything new!" Then he said, "Write this down, for these
words are trustworthy and true."[5]

I am sure that my brief description of God's workings is a
hopelessly impoverished version of the real thing, seeing it as I
do with my finite mind through the knothole of time and space.
Yet even these fragments boggle the mind. They make us realize
that the ladders we are climbing just may be leaning against the
wrong buildings. If God is making something new, and if we are
in the middle of His plan, there must be some major implications
for us and for the way we live life.

YOUR PART OF THE ACTION IN GOD'S PURPOSES

God does have purposes for us. Some of them are for the future,
but others are for the present. I find it astonishing that the Creator
has chosen to partner with us, His creation, in this work that He
is doing. But that is what the Bible says.

If anyone is in Christ, he is a new creation; the old has
gone, the new has come! All this is from God, who recon-
ciled us to himself through Christ and gave us the ministry
of reconciliation. . . . We are therefore Christ's ambassa-
dors, as though God were making his appeal through us.[6]

By including us, God has given us another of His great gifts:
purposefulness. How is it that we so often manage to drain the
sense of awe and adventure out of this involvement with God as
His "fellow workers"?[7] We even manage to turn it into something
tedious, reducing it to routines we can scarcely endure.

I know Christians who get more satisfaction out of their

careers than they do out of their participation with God in His work. How can it be that the Dow Chemical Corporation can solicit and get the best of our creative energies to the point where there is really nothing left over for this eternal enterprise we are talking about? God's call should make every other voice sound frail and tentative by comparison.

In this section we will briefly examine three calls that God makes to us. As we respond to them, we should find ourselves purposefully engaged in His eternal enterprise.

CALLED TO CITIZENSHIP IN GOD'S KINGDOM

We are told to "live lives that are worthy of God, who calls us into his kingdom and glory."[8]

God is our king. We are citizens of His kingdom, members of His household.[9] That is our present reality.

This call to kingdom citizenship is a radical call. When Jesus was before Pilate, He said, "My kingdom is not of this world."[10] This is a provocative, far-reaching statement.

If His Kingdom is not of this world and we are of His Kingdom, then the rules by which we operate will be different. We will not live as the world lives. For example, we will not resort to the recourses of the world to deal with the issues of our day. Many of us are ignoring this. We have chosen the lower road. We are resorting to the same political mechanisms our opponents use to express their convictions. We demonstrate, boycott, and lobby along with everyone else, making ourselves ugly in the eyes of those who oppose us. We are ugly because our actions are based on judgment rather than mercy. A Kingdom citizen feeds his enemy, and if his enemy is thirsty he gives him something to drink! He overcomes evil with good.[11] He gets there first to bring healing. This is a powerful way to respond and yet it is something we have all but lost.

Citizenship in the Kingdom brings purpose even to the routine affairs of life. It obliterates the artificial line we are so prone to draw between the secular and the spiritual. We are citizens twenty-four hours a day, so we represent the Kingdom all the time, in everything we do. In this world we are expatriates, foreigners. We live as insiders among people who often have no notion that life could possibly be different for them, that there exists another option for living. So whatever we may be doing—caring for our homes, disciplining our children, meeting a deadline for our boss, or taking a vacation—we need to remember that we are at the same time making a statement about what it means to belong to God.

The Kingdom of God banishes the mundane. Meaning is everywhere in every action.

CALLED TO BECOME A NEW WATERING HOLE

The second call we are considering comes from Jesus.

> On the last and greatest day of the Feast, Jesus stood and said in a loud voice, "If anyone is thirsty, let him come to me and drink. Whoever believes in me, as the Scripture has said, streams of living water will flow from within him."[12]

That must have been quite a scene. The town square was thronged with people, the festivities were in full swing, with plenty to eat and drink for everyone. Then Jesus stood up and offered to quench everyone's thirst!

One can get very thirsty at a party where there is plenty to drink. Jesus knew that. He understood this thirst of ours and He referred to it often. The woman at the well had been attempting to quench her thirst for years and had gone through five husbands in her search.[13] Jesus offered to quench that thirst. He told her almost the same thing He told the crowd at the feast: that she would not only never thirst, but she would have "a spring of water welling up to external life."[14] She would have water to spare.

We do not need to belabor the point. We have all experienced this thirst, this dissatisfaction, this yearning for something more that sometimes seems to be unquenchable. And like the woman at the well, we are prone to look in all the wrong places.

We go for the glitz. It's the American way. We have been raised to believe that the bigger something is, the faster it goes or grows and the more it costs, the better it is. This is how we define success, whether it's a business, sports, or a new movie. We give little value to the small or the obscure.

Jesus was obscure. When He came there was "nothing in his appearance that we should desire him."[15] He was so nondescript that the world did not recognize Him, even though He made it all.[16] He told His followers that they would be of the same making.[17]

Given our orientation, it is no surprise that we could miss the very things that are the most thirst-quenching. Drinking from Christ Himself and having water to spare for others gives great satisfaction. Jesus Himself received such satisfaction from His conversation with a woman who was insignificant among her own people that He forgot His own hunger. He explained, "My food . . . is to do the will of him who sent me and to finish his work."[18]

My dad is eighty-five years old. I visited him not long ago. He picked me up at the airport, and on our way to his house we stopped for lunch at his favorite restaurant. As we ate I asked him how he was doing. He replied that he was living the best days of his life, that he was so motivated he could hardly wait to get up in the morning.

Now that's a rather unusual response from someone of Dad's age. Often life becomes a burden for people who are eighty-something. Their days can become long and vacant. So I asked Dad what he was up to. He told me about the people in his life: the young couple about to be married, the nightclub bouncer. The list went on and on. His life is filled with people who are finding Christ and growing in Him. I asked him where he finds them all. Some he meets while on his daily walk. One of his favorite spots is the Jacuzzi at the health club. But generally it's one person leading him to others.

It wasn't always that way with Dad. He became a Christian while he was in his twenties. From the start he was serious about following Christ and he did his best to teach his children to do the same. He has been an elder in his church for as long as I can remember. He would share his faith with people, but little would come of it because his vision revolved around, and was limited to, the activities in the church.

In 1971 my parents visited us in Brazil where we were working as missionaries with students and young professionals. Our first generation of believers was just coming to maturity and beginning to multiply at that time. One by one, over the days my parents were with us, these young Christians would tell their stories. Finally Dad came to me. He said, "I've never seen young Christians like these before. What are you doing to get them to grow like this?"

I didn't know how to answer so I suggested he just watch and see. So Dad watched, and saw nothing. He saw nothing because we weren't doing anything that he could recognize as a religious activity. The familiar forms weren't there: no formal meetings, no services. We were doing everything on an individual and small-group basis. I was unaware of how different this was from what my dad was accustomed to until he commented on it. We were simply doing the things that fit the situation.

Dad and I discussed his observations as he was preparing to return home. He could see how the things we were doing in Curitiba, Brazil, could serve to reach his unbelieving friends in Crystal, Minnesota. He went home and reordered his life. Scores of people have met Christ and have grown to maturity in Dad's living room over these past twenty years. He has become the consummate insider.

Our fascination with bigness makes it easy to believe that ministering as an insider among a few "not very important people" isn't really very interesting. It seems slow, obscure, and the outcome seems dubious. Our problem is that we tend to look at God's enterprise with our earthbound eyes. But when the fruit begins to come, we can understand why Jesus forgot His hunger and why the Apostle John penned the words, "I have no greater joy than to hear that my children are walking in the truth."[19]

It is worth the effort to learn to serve as a watering hole for others.

CALLED TO TAKE IT TO THE WORLD

Can you imagine being among the eleven who met with Jesus on that mountain in Galilee after He had risen from the dead? Jesus instructed them to go to all the nations and teach people in these nations everything He had taught them.[20]

If any of the eleven did any quick math on the spot, they would have wondered if Jesus was serious. He had spent something over three years instructing them. Now he was telling them to repeat what He had done with them among every people on earth!

Think of the magnitude of that assignment, and of what it would cost those men, personally!

But Jesus could not have said what He said here if He had not done what He did during His years of ministry. His primary task had been to prepare that small audience to receive those few words. He reveals this in His prayer to His Father in John 17. There He tells His Father that He had completed the work the Father had given Him to do.[21] That "work," we find, was to bring those eleven into an intimate knowledge of the Father so that they would know what to do when they went to the nations. They would know how to draw on the authority, power, and glory of the Father.[22]

Those men could go because Jesus had put them through His school of faith, and because as they went, Jesus Himself would pray for them. He gave them the Holy Spirit, and with Him access to all of the authority of Christ.

Jesus was thinking generations when He gave that command to the eleven. He did not expect them to get to every breathing soul on earth. They would reach some, and these in turn would reach others—until the world would hear. He prayed, "My prayer is not for them alone [the eleven]. I pray also for those who will believe in me through their message. . . . May they also be in us so that the world may believe that you have sent me."[23]

Again we have the characteristic pattern of the kingdom at work: low profile, low maintenance, no need for press coverage, just go to people. And they did it.

It is still the best way. My work has to do with establishing the gospel in places where it hasn't gone or where its voice is weak. The best possible approach to starting something new in a country is to send in a pair of mature, tested couples who will think long-term. They will learn the language and put their roots down. It may take them the rest of their lives before they see fruit that is bearing fruit. That kind of beginning is slow and obscure, but in the long run it will outstrip and outlast any other more gala approach to missions.

Some of you need to give this call of Christ serious consideration. You may need to start packing. Most of us need to remain as insiders in our present situation—but this does not exclude us from global opportunities.

We who belong to Christ are part of a global household, or family. Whatever our nationality or culture, we are sons and daughters of the same Father and stand to share in the same eternal inheritance. We enjoy a common kinship and it doesn't take long for that to become evident when we find ourselves together.

I am traveling as I write this, returning from an encounter with believers who are laboring in the Muslim countries. I had never met many of the people I was with before and language differences often kept our verbal communication at a minimum. But there were tears as we parted. The common bond in Christ is very strong.

I believe we all need to maintain some vital connections with what God is doing among the nations. This is not the place to expand greatly on the forms this might take. I will restrict my comments to just a couple of ideas.

As a rule our participation in missions is impersonal and indirect. We give some money to the missions fund and we have an annual missions conference where we learn something of what's going on in a few places in the world. But I have observed that it takes direct, personal participation with people who live and labor in other parts of the world for the reality of our being members of a global family to sink in.

In 1970 a couple of friends who were supporting us financially visited us in Brazil. At the end of their visit, as they were leaving, one of them confided in me. He said, "I have the ability to give, but I'm frustrated because there isn't much going on that I enjoy giving my money to. I want you to know that if you need anything, I'll be there to meet it."

I looked at my friend and realized that he needed the opportunity I could provide for him, and that I needed the kind of backing he was offering. We really needed one another. Over the succeeding years this person met need after need as they arose. His involvement went far beyond giving. He became a part of our ministry, made friends with many. He taught others how to manage their own finances and how to support their own ministries. Our colaborship has expanded into other areas as well and we continue to live in dependence on one another. It has been a mutually enriching relationship.

I have some other friends who have spent their lives designing and constructing buildings. They desire to use their professional experience and financial resources to serve others in this global family that belongs to Christ. So I connected them with a couple in Africa, both of whom are medical doctors. After doing specializations in foreign medical school, this African couple had returned to their country for the sake of taking the gospel to their people. They need a clinic to work in. These two friends of mine are currently working directly with this couple to build the clinic. I know lifetime friendships are being forged. It is impossible to say who is going to benefit most from this effort.

SUMMARY

As insiders we participate in God's work by responding to three calls:

- To live as worthy citizens of God's Kingdom.
- To become new watering holes for others.
- To maintain a live connection with others in the global family.

As we grow in these three areas we will find our lives taking on new dimensions of meaning.

NOTES
1. Ephesians 1:3-14, 2:9-12.
2. Habakkuk 1:3-4.
3. Habakkuk 2:14.
4. Psalm 2:7-8; Daniel 7:17-18; 1 Corinthians 15:20-29; Ephesians 2:19-22; Colossians 1:15-20; Revelation 5:9-10, 12:7-17.
5. Revelation 21:3-5.
6. 2 Corinthians 5:17-20.
7. 2 Corinthians 6:1.
8. 1 Thessalonians 2:12.
9. Ephesians 2:19.
10. John 18:36.
11. Romans 12:20-21.
12. John 7:37-38.
13. John 4:18.
14. John 4:14.
15. Isaiah 53:2.
16. John 1:10.
17. John 15:20-21.
18. John 4:34.
19. 3 John 4.
20. Matthew 28:16-20.
21. John 17:4.
22. John 17:6-19.
23. John 17:20-21.

CHAPTER 13

The Time War: Creating Margin

T his final chapter may be the most important part of this book. We have laid out a vision for how we can participate with God in the work He is doing, primarily as insiders to our natural networks of friends and acquaintances. We talked about the goals of such a ministry, and the responsibilities. We saw that there are things we must learn and skills we need to acquire if we are to be competent.

As we have proceeded through this book I can imagine you, the reader, becoming increasingly uncomfortable over a question growing in the back of your mind. Finally it surfaces: "Where am I going to find time for these things? I'm back there in chapter 2! You know, I'm the person whose hands are full just coping with his own private chaos. I simply have no time to even think about the things you're talking about, much less do them."

There are many things that can keep us from responding to God's call to become fellow workers with Him, but for those of us in this chaotic society of ours, this time crunch is truly a major impediment. There are no easy answers, so the temptation is for us to just forget the whole idea.

What we need is margin.

MARGIN

I have taken this term from a book written by Richard Swenson, M.D. I recommend that you read it as it is an extensive treatment of the subject we are addressing here.

Margin, says Swenson, "is the leeway we once had between ourselves and our limits."[1] It is the extra space between the things we must do and our capacity. When we use up all of that space, we are working at full capacity and there is no margin left. Then, when extra demands come or something unexpected arises, we suffer overload. We feel harassed, suffer stress, and experience all sorts of negative effects on our health and our emotions.

As a medical doctor, Swenson found himself attending a parade of patients whose basic problem was really overload. He concludes, "Something *is* wrong. People are tired and frazzled. People are anxious and depressed. People don't have time to heal anymore. There is a psychic instability in our day that prevents peace from implanting itself very firmly in the human spirit. And despite the skeptics, this instability is not the same old nemesis recast in a modern role. What we have here is a brand new disease."[2]

Swenson enumerates a long list of overloads that cause us pain. We can be overloaded with activities, with choices, commitments, debts, education, expectations, fatigue, information, media, ministry, people, work, traffic, and on and on.[3] Chronically overloaded people lose their capacity to respond. Often they are misunderstood as being weak, apathetic, or lacking in commitment.

Swenson found himself living without margin. He struggled with the alternatives for a couple of years and then he took a radical step: He cut his medical practice in half. His recommendation is, "Add a dose of margin and see if life doesn't come alive once again."[4]

This problem of overload and lack of margin is a threat to more than just our health and sanity. It also threatens to frustrate the very purpose for our existence! Most people race through life at full throttle, headed in no particular direction at all. Someday they will stand before God and explain, "We really wanted to be more involved with You, Lord, but You know how things were at the job. And with both of us working, the kids needed extra activities. We felt like we lived in our cars, running them back and forth. It all seemed so important. . . ."

Either we take the initiative and resume control over our circumstances, or that will be our story as we stand before God.

Resisting the Centrifugal Forces

One of our daughters got married a couple of years ago. Both she and her husband are still in college, both studying business and economics. They are both artistic. Our daughter's artistic outlet is film making; our son-in-law composes music and sings with a group. So, film shoots and music rehearsals devour time.

I watched our fledgling couple with interest to see what would happen. Sure enough, it didn't take very many months before they began to express some sense of loss in their relationship. It is inevitable that if one party in a marriage pursues one consuming interest and the other pursues another, the space that they once shared together will eventually become empty.

Fortunately, we were around to catch this and help them reorient themselves. Many young couples continue their separate pursuits until they discover there is little or nothing left to keep them together.

I believe this absence of a common purpose is the beginning of the malaise of overload and loss of margin. As life goes on, as children, responsibilities, and acquisitions increase, the pull toward disintegration also increases. It costs money to live, so we have to work. As the job evolves into a career, it takes on added significance. It provides not just groceries, but status as well. Soon both husband and wife are busy pursuing careers.

When children come, they need day care. Next come piano lessons, little league baseball, drama classes, and a myriad of other activities to keep them occupied while dad and mom are working.

Church activities also take a lot of time, as does everything else in life, sending the family in as many directions as there are family members.

Our social relationships have the same scattering effect on the family.

The sad fact is that everything in our lives works like a centrifugal force that would dismember the family in a flurry of activities—and leave nothing but an empty hole at the center. To illustrate:

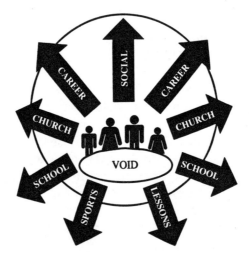

Certain things become obvious here. It is obvious that if this family does not act to change their situation, their ties to one another will weaken and continue to lose meaning. It is also obvious that it is up to them to take the necessary action to regain control of their lives. They need to decide what their lives should revolve around, what common purposes and values should characterize them as a family. They need to agree on how they are going to live life together.

This will not be easy. It will require some hard choices. We can't have it all. A choice for one thing is automatically a choice against something else.

The Sweet Song of the Siren of Modernity

One of modernity's themes is, "You owe it to yourself to achieve your full potential." That sounds good, almost Christian, doesn't it? But it's a lie that will tear you apart and leave you with nothing. Pursuing it will put unbearable pressure on your marriage. And you certainly won't sign on to partner with God in His work in this world if you are listening to this refrain.

Jesus said, "I tell you the truth, unless a kernel of wheat falls to the ground and dies, it remains only a single seed. But if it dies, it produces many seeds. The man who loves his life will lose it."[5] Really, you won't get far in reordering your life and recovering margin until you silence modernity's song and replace it with these words of Jesus.

The spirit of modernity makes the things I am talking about especially difficult to accept.

Regaining Control Over Your Life

It will take work—deliberate, conscious effort—and it will take time to regain margin and find the space to be available in your calling as an insider. You will become a nonconformist.

Why not begin with a private weekend retreat? Put it on your calendar and begin to prepare for it. Do it with your spouse, and then later with your children. If you're single, go with a friend that shares the same needs and desires.

Get away from home and your familiar surroundings, from telephones and people who know you. Spend the first day in the Scriptures, in prayer, and in personal assessment. Decide what should be central to your life. Devote the second day to working through and examining the commitments that make up your life. Ask yourself how they contribute to or work against the things you want your life to be about.

Begin the second day by reviewing the eternal perspective on your life. The message of 2 Corinthians 4:16-5:10 can help you do that.

One of the most fundamental differences between a Christian and a nonChristian is the factor of hope. Paul wrote, "You were . . . without hope and without God in the world."[6] A person without hope looks at life from the perspective of the seventy-odd years he can expect to live. It looks like this:

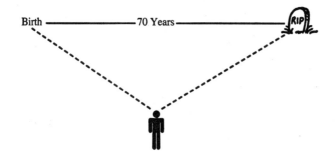

As life moves on for the person who carries this perspective, he becomes more and more anxious. His 40th birthday is a full-blown crisis. "It's more than half over," he worries. Since all he can see is the few waning years, he becomes increasingly concerned about getting the most out of what's left. The more anxious he becomes, the more selfish and erratic he gets.

The Resurrection changes this perspective for us. Peter writes, "In his great mercy [God] has given us new birth into a living hope through the resurrection of Jesus Christ from the dead."[7] The Resurrection injects eternity into the picture. When Jesus rose from the dead, He showed us what is on the other side of the grave and also paved the way for us into eternity. So our perspective has been revolutionized!

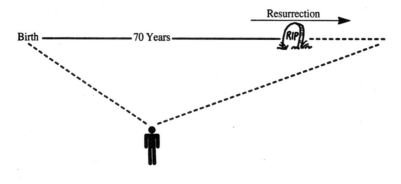

This new perspective transforms our attitude toward both time and life. Do I have time? I have eternity! So what if I don't get to do all the things I'd enjoy doing? I don't have to. There's more beyond!

If we ignore this eternal perspective, we will certainly write the wrong answer in that circle marked "void."

After reflecting on these things, ask yourself some questions and write down your answers. Let me suggest a few:

- "What are the key Scripture passages that God has used in my life in the past?" Go back and review them. Ask yourself if they still carry the same influence over your life and thought as they did when they were new to you.
- "Do I know Christ more intimately now than I did a year ago? In what ways? How did it happen?"
- "What motives, positive and negative, drive my life? What does this tell me about what's at the center of my life?"
- "What anxieties do I experience? What causes them? How do I deal with them? How should I be dealing with them?"
- "What should be central to my life? What do I think God wants me to be and do?"
- "What commitments occupy my time? (job, programs, activities, relationships, etc.). What changes need to be made in these areas? How am I going to do this?"

One idea that can greatly simplify an overloaded life is to consolidate several purposes into a single activity. Read Romans 16 with this idea in mind. In the early centuries of Christianity almost everything happened in homes. So when the church met, it was one's own family, together with the neighbors and their families. A spectrum of needs was met in a single experience.

We can't return to the first century, but we can take some lessons from it. Relationships are what make life worth living, beginning with one's relationship with God and extending into one's family, friends, and on out. Relationships take time. They need to be cultivated regularly. The more we can integrate our relation-ships, the more we can achieve a convergence in our spiritual, social, and recreational needs, the simpler our lives will become.

I have a number of spiritually mature Christian friends and colleagues that I love and enjoy very much. The most natural thing in the world would be for me to build my social life around these relationships. But we live in a world full of lost people and my Christian friends already have what I can offer to others. So I tell them—and myself—that we'll get caught up in Heaven.

It takes time to turn things around in a life that has become overloaded. I am in the midst of this process myself and I'm find-ing that it's not easy to work my way out of one set of commit-ments and into the new. For me, things had to get worse before they could get better. One can't just walk away from things. It takes time.

It also takes persistence. If you spend a weekend now working through your commitments and priorities, you will need to set a date for six months later to review your decisions and your prog-ress. In fact, one of the best decisions you could make would be to take a day, or a weekend, every six months to reflect on the issues we are discussing here, and to regroup so that your life will stay on track in relation to your calling.

CONCLUSION

Our walk with Christ is meant to be an adventure. But surrounded as we are by the pressures of our modern society, it's not easy to keep the adventure alive. In the course of this book we have explored the elements that need to be present if the adventure is to endure. They can be summarized in the few statements that follow:

- Each of us is called to a living bond with Christ. This relationship is to be a two-way street between Him and us. As we heed His Word and engage Him in our daily affairs, He engages us as well in His.
- We are also called into a living bond with one another.

This implies that we are a safe place for each other to come to, where God empowers us to walk in truth and to overcome the things that have us in bondage.

■ We can participate in the eternal purposes of God, whatever our situation. We are called to glorify God among the people who make up our networks of relationships. We should be looking to God to make us fruitful in the various contexts where we live out our lives.

■ The Great Commission is really God's invitation to us to colabor with Him in accomplishing His purposes among the nations. All of us, in some way, at some level, need to respond to this call.

NOTES

1. Richard Swenson, M.D., *Margin* (Colorado Springs, CO: NavPress, 1992), page 92.
2. Swenson, page 17.
3. Swenson, pages 83-87.
4. Swenson, page 91.
5. John 12:24-25.
6. Ephesians 2:12.
7. 1 Peter 1:3.

Author

In 1963 Jim Petersen and his wife, Marge, pioneered the Navigator work in Brazil among unchurched university students. Throughout the years, this has grown into a lay movement that continues to expand.

By 1973 the foundations were laid in Brazil, and new generations of leaders were building on them. Jim turned his attention to other Latin American countries, recruiting missionary teams and coaching them in their efforts. He served as Latin America director for The Navigators until 1985, when the Petersens moved to Colorado Springs, Colorado, where The Navigators' international headquarters is located. The move was precipitated by Jim's growing international involvement outside Latin America.

In 1988 Jim began leading an international leadership development project, the Scriptural Roots of Ministry (SRM). The purpose of the SRM is to equip a ministry team to resolve their own issues through biblical research and by working out practical answers in the field. He travels extensively to various countries when invited to help others work through this process. Jim is currently part of a four-man executive team that leads the international work of The Navigators.

Jim brings the fruit of his lifetime of experience into his writing. He has written *Living Proof*—a video series under the same title is also available—and *Church Without Walls*. This book, *Lifestyle Discipleship*, although it stands alone, is a further development of what he has written in his previous works.